JOURNEY OF A LIFETIME

THOMAS MATUS

ISBN: 978-1-962402-24-8

Published by

Fideli Publishing, Inc.
119 W. Morgan St.
Martinsville, IN 46151
www.FideliPublishing.com

Thanks to
Paula Huston

Preface

I first met Fr. Thomas Matus in the ancient monastery of Camaldoli in the Appennine mountains of Italy. I was among a group of oblates on a pilgrimage led by two Camaldolese monks from one of their American daughter houses—Incarnation Monastery in Berkeley, California. We had arrived in Rome late on the evening of September 10, 2002. The next morning, we jet-lagged travelers were brought to tears during Mass at San Gregorio al Celio, the Camaldolese house on the Caelian Hill in front of the Palatine, when the monks there prayed fervently for America on the one-year anniversary of 9/11.

Though Fr. Thomas was himself American—a Californian, in fact—many years before, he'd opted to make his stability in the 1,000-year-old motherhouse. By now, he was not only fluent in Italian, he *was* Italian—at least, this is how he seemed to me. Charged with guiding us during our days at the ancient cenobium, he spoke with a relaxed Italian elegance, taking time for plenty of delightful side—trails, but also conveying a depth of knowledge and monastic wisdom I hadn't encountered before.

I soon found myself seeking him out during breaks, where I peppered him with questions—not only about Camaldolese history but about my own spiritual struggles as a fairly new convert to Catholicism. Though at first, he seemed a bit nonplussed—my sense was that he was more used to teaching young monks than he was to advising earnest female inquirers—he was patiently attentive, and I left Italy with the sense that I'd made a new friend in the monastic community.

I didn't see Fr. Thomas again for some years. Then I heard he'd returned to America and was living at the Berkeley house. And then, finally, he was back at New Camaldoli Hermitage in Big Sur, where he'd first come as a postulant in the early sixties and where he'd made his monastic profession—New

Camaldoli, where he once thought he'd be spending the rest of his life.

In 2018, he led another pilgrimage to Italy, this one called "In the Steps of St. Romuald of Ravenna." My husband and I were among the group, and by then, I was already immersed in research for my book *The Hermits of Big Sur*, a history of the 1958 Camaldolese California foundation. I'd not yet had a chance to talk with Fr. Thomas about the project, and our leisurely journey through Florence, Ravenna, Venice, Camaldoli and Rome gave me the opportunity to sit beside him during many meals. I realized that this erudite monk was a key source of historical, cultural, and theological information about the Camaldolese, and I asked if he'd be willing to help me with the book.

During the following year, I made numerous trips to New Camaldoli, where I met with Fr. Thomas for hours at a time amid clouds of book dust in the hermitage archives, a window-less, L-shaped closet lit by flickering fluorescent bulbs. Though close to eighty by then, he was indefatigable. Even better for my project, within him burned the heart of a Sherlock

Holmes. For the early days of New Camaldoli were shadowed in mystery—a sixty-year-old mystery by then—and none of the original pioneers who might have been able to shed light were still alive except for him.

Together, we read countless Italian letters from the late fifties and early sixties, with Fr. Thomas translating on the fly. I was fascinated and so was he. And slowly, we pieced together what had happened. As it turned out, something different than he'd surmised sixty years before as a novice in his very early twenties.

If I'd ever needed evidence that the monastic life is a transformative one, this moment of realization that he'd been wrong back then was it. He'd been so very sure. He'd held on to his theory for decades. He was positive he'd figured out who was at fault and who was an innocent victim. But what we'd uncovered did not support his long-held theory, so, without a moment's hesitation, he let it go. Not only that, but right there in the book dust, he confessed to me that he'd harbored unjust thoughts and was heartily sorry for all of them.

I don't think I'd ever encountered such readiness to admit a failure of judgment, much less such honest contrition. What made the moment even more remarkable was Fr. Thomas's age. As we get older, we tend to cling even more stubbornly to long-held notions. Here, in contrast, was a man forever young—a monk always willing to learn from his own mistakes so that he might keep growing.

This is the Fr. Thomas Matus I've come to love and admire. His brilliant mind and depth of learning are in a class by themselves, and I never tire of hearing what he might teach me next. But it's his Benedictine humility that catches at my heart. As he would be the first to admit, it hasn't been always easy being him. There are times he's felt like the odd man out—the unusual character nobody quite "gets." Yet he's never wavered in his commitment to obedience, both to his brothers in Christ, and to God himself. And because of this deep commitment, made so young, he's become a gift to the whole monastic community—both in Italy and America—and a fully flourishing human being besides: a true exemplar of the Camaldolese "Three-Fold Good."

When I encouraged him to tell the story of his earliest years, he was at first reluctant, telling me he didn't feel right about calling attention to his personal history. I told him that people need to hear conversion stories like his—that they might be inspired to make a serious spiritual search of their own. So, without further ado, he got to work, solemnly declaring that he was writing the following "under obedience" to his friend Paula.

I couldn't be more tickled.

Paula Huston
March 4, 2025
New Camaldoli Hermitage

Thomas Matus, *monachus et musicus,*
necnon et eremita beandus, monk
and musician and even a happy hermit

Foreword

"I talk to Dear God,"
— Wladyslava Klepacka Matusiewicza
(my grandmother on my father's side,
as she told me how she prayed)

God listens to souls, whether they speak to God with the words of any known language or with a wordless language. Your prayer can be in a language that you may not know from A to Z, whether English, Esperanto, French, Italian, Latin, or Polish. God does not make you pray. God has made every heart that prays, especially the heart of a child, one who doesn't yet know how to pray but rather sighs more deeply than words can say. For me, when as a child I started to pray, I realized that my prayer was mine but not totally mine. No one told me to pray, but a few, like my mother, did teach me some prayers. And my Polish grandmother told me I could talk to Dear God whenever I wanted to.

I ask myself a question: "If I didn't live in a monastery, could I still live with my dilemmas in an institutional Church?" I can and do say yes, but the yes I live by is said in a monastery. The "yes" is said to my monastic sisters and brothers, and it refers to the life of rules and vows that for us Benedictines begin with stability, then continue with the reforming of our lives, and ultimately conclude with obeying the sighs in our souls that are too deep for anyone to say.

The individual soul is what she is, but only if she is with other souls. All this is taking place now, in our Church, as she explores her path together with Pope Francis. He bears witness to a Church in transformation. The Church that once called herself *Mater et Magistra,* "Mother and Teacher," now fosters a synodal choir that sings, no longer in the range of baritones and tenors alone, but also with contraltos and sopranos and *voci bianche* whose voices rise above them all, because they are the youngest and their voices stand out among the others.

These are new times, when we find a Church that is both catholic and synodal, less uniform and more and more a varied people of God walking together, among whom we elders must now blend in harmony with all the voices in the choral Church, chiefly the younger who walk ahead of us. In a family we find both old and young, both tall and small, but we don't need to explain anything to anyone, just welcome them and let them learn how it's done. We learn to sing by singing; we learn to pray by praying.

The church's new wardrobe is no longer cut and sewn for tall and broad-shouldered humanity alone. While the new style and cut may seem more casual and less formal than yesterday's garb, it serves better to keep us warm. And then there is the one thing that we must faithfully do: keep saying "yes" to the desire and the conscious intention to sew and wear articles of clothing that are not uniform, that instead fit every size and shape, according to the pattern of our human nature. These garments were worn by the One Who Is, in the Person of the only begotten Son of a virgin Mother. She is everyone's mother, and I am sure she loves the various colors of her children's clothing.

PART ONE
THE EARLY YEARS

Chapter 1

We all have stories to tell about ourselves and our loved ones, about public events and personal memories. But no human individual can have in mind a direct visual image of her or his own birth; one may perhaps have photographic images of the newborn child or children. These I do have, since my father owned a camera store on Wilshire Boulevard, within the "miracle mile" of Hollywood, California.

Yes, Hollywood, the "Mecca of cinema," was my birthplace. To this very day—halfway into my eighties—I am more than ever conscious of the circumstances of my birth and of the cultural values represented by my hometown. Any one film may be ill-conceived or trivial, but the arts of movie-making and the artists, whether great or less than great, who have crafted the culture of cinema, have given me a terrain upon which I have followed God's call to become a monk and a Catholic priest, hoping to be of service to others, some of whom, like me, had grown up with movies and whose understanding of human life has been illuminated by the projected light of films.

Up to now I have kept my father's photo albums and films together with other mementos, including the oral history narrated by my parents, about the circumstances of my birth and about the cultural importance of the urban environment where I first opened my eyes. Any film shot in Hollywood might have its intrinsic artistic and spiritual value, but the real masters of the art of cinema seem to have opened a space for me to hear God's voice and to embrace a contemplative life. At this point in my life, I hope that I have lived this life well and have been of service to others whom I have met on my path, some who, like me, have been guided in some way by the light of films.

My father, Anthony Thomas Matus (1904–1968), was a son of Polish immigrants and was called "Tony" by family members and friends. His parents met in New York City shortly after they had arrived from different parts of Poland, and they quickly married. Tony was their second son and showed signs of intelligence and musical talent. Attending public school, he earned high marks. After eighth grade, his father wanted him to go to work, but Tony begged his mother to let him finish high school: "What if I am called to be a priest?" he said to his mother. "The seminary won't accept me, if I haven't finished school." Although my grandmother knew that her second son had no calling to the priesthood, she argued with Grandfather, who always respected her aristocratic origins and usually acceded to her preferences. Tony finished high school and then took courses in accounting at a business college.

My mother was Clara Mae Agee (1910–1990), a distant cousin of the short-lived poet, novelist and film writer James Agee. I was her only child. Her nickname, "Boots," was borrowed from a comic strip, "Boots and her Buddies," about a young lady who went to college hoping either to become a professor or to marry a professor. Born in Fort Worth, Texas, she was given her nickname during the academic year 1926–1927 at Oklahoma Christian University, then called Oklahoma Baptist University. Boots' mother, Minna Myrtle Stevenson, was taking courses to qualify as an elementary school teacher, and my mother's sister Vera Lee—nicknamed "Billee" and just barely a year older than Boots—was attending the same courses. During that year Boots earned her high school diploma along with some college credits. What Boots was aiming for was simpler: to graduate from high school and to earn a few college credits besides, and in addition she needed the skills of a secretary.

Boots' mother had separated from Arthur Francis Agee, the father of the two girls. Arthur had been a Baptist preacher whose friendly relations with some ladies in his church had stirred up gossip and got him fired from the pulpit. Some of the devout also claimed that he had taken to drink. Billee and Boots did not believe the gossip about their father, but they were happy to join their mother in Oklahoma, sharing as they did her desire for a good education. But after her year at O.C.U., my mother did not go for a college degree. The Depression soon destroyed the world's economy, and Boots, in view of finding a job, attended a secretarial school and became exceptionally proficient in stenography and typing. Her sister went to California and married a Catholic. While not embracing his faith, she did allow him to raise their children as Catholics.

My parents met in 1934, deep in the Depression. Both were employed by Joseph Froggat at his life insurance firm in Los Angeles. My mother was Mr. Froggat's private secretary, and Tony was gifted in elaborating actuarial tables; these skills gained him steady employment in those days before computers. After several months of dating and, having fallen very much in love, Boots and Tony exchanged their vows in Hollywood's Baptist church on May 4, 1935, and enjoyed their brief honeymoon at a California desert oasis. Boots was not a virgin and so had chosen not to wear white at their wedding, but with Tony's consent, they had observed premarital chastity until their wedding night.

A year into their marriage, Boots suffered a miscarriage that ended her first pregnancy. During her second, the one that produced me, she and Tony would sometimes speak directly to me, telling me to stay in there until I was completely ready to come out into the bright Southern California sunlight. During her pregnancy, I was their audience as they sang, *"You are my sunshine, my only sunshine...,"* along with other current hits and golden oldies. Even though Tony had not learned to read music, he had an excellent musical ear and a fine, second-tenor voice, having briefly been trained by a professional singing coach. Boots had taken music lessons, including some training in piano and violin, but she never wished to perform in public, not even to accompany hymns in church. Nonetheless, I was born into what I would call, without a moment's hesitation, a musical family.

A certain Mr. Craig, one of Tony's friends in Hollywood, had a successful business named "Craig Movie Supply Company," specializing in equipment used for editing films. Tony had long wanted to have his own business, and in 1938 he opened a camera store, which he called "Matus Camera Supply Company," one door away from the corner of Wilshire Boulevard and La Brea Avenue, and near to several movie studios. This was in the heart of what was called "the miracle mile" and a short walk from the Hollywood Biltmore Hotel, where famous actors would stay during the shooting of their films.

One of these actors, a gorgeous starlet named Rhonda Fleming, came into Tony's store in search of film for her rare camera, and Tony, who had been careful to stock every available kind of camera film, had exactly what she needed. After paying for the roll of film she walked out, but then Tony realized that she had not taken the change for her purchase. So, he ran out of the store, calling out: "Miss Fleming, Miss Fleming, you forgot your change!" and caught up with her. She thanked him for his honesty and told him that anyone else would have kept the change for himself. That evening, Tony shared the story with Boots, and they had a good laugh.

Chapter 2

On February 22, 1940, I came forth into this world in an urban area of Los Angeles County called West Hollywood, just outside the L.A. city limits. It was not incorporated but an area carved out to accommodate Samuel Goldwyn's movie studio and to exempt him from city taxes. At about 4 a.m. Boots' water broke, and Tony drove her to the closest maternity hospital, the one near Mr. Goldwyn's studio. There, at 2:04 p.m., I opened my blue eyes to the light of a rainy day, with baby teeth starting to emerge from my gums, abundant golden-blond hair on my head and complex lines on the palms of both hands, signs that I was indeed a post-mature baby, whose birth took place a couple of weeks beyond the usual nine months of pregnancy.

Looking back on my perinatal memories, it seems to me that I had a certain degree of consciousness during the last phase of gestation, even before the beginning of my life outside the womb. I had been hearing the affectionate words the lovers shared and the love songs they sang together, and the beginning of my life outside Boots' womb was enriched by dreams that evoked my awareness of living within her.

My parents called me "Russell"; my birth certificate named me Russell Anthony Matus. I took my father's confirmation name "Thomas" when, in 1961, I was confirmed in a Catholic parish on the outskirts of Los Angeles. The following year, I became a monk at New Camaldoli Hermitage in Big Sur, California, and I decided to profess my Benedictine vows as "Thomas."

Many years later, as a monk in our Big Sur hermitage, I met Dr. Stanislav Grof and enjoyed many conversations with him, with his late wife Christina and with other colleagues, who gathered for month-long conferences at Esalen Institute, just 8.7 miles (14 km.) north of New Camaldoli. Grof had earned both an M.D. and a Ph.D. in his native land, the Czech Republic, where he practiced Freudian psychoanalysis. After emigrating to the United States, Grof joined with colleagues who, like himself, were developing new paradigms of human consciousness and a new practice of psychoanalysis through the study of dreams and extraordinary psychic experiences, often employing non-addictive psychoactive substances (e.g. LSD), alongside intensive breath work.

With these new paradigms Grof and his colleagues were able to analyze and convincingly interpret perinatal dreams (dreams of coming to birth), like those I have experienced. For example, when I was twelve, I dreamed the following: I am in space, coming in for a landing on earth; I am not on a spaceship but in a space suit. I have difficulty in achieving the proper trajectory, and only on the third try am I able to land. As I touch down, my life support system flips over my head, and the air tube twists around my neck, but fortunately I am able to pull it away. The backpack that precedes my landing would be, according to Grof's interpretive methodology, an appropriate image of a *placenta-praevia* birth, which in my case, fortunately, did not hinder my first breath. I have retained other vivid memories, like a brief vision from an out-of-body viewpoint in the hospital room where Boots was recovering.

Another dream also included a very early childhood memory, dating back to before my first birthday: a dream of myself, lying in a perambulator under a bright sun. Psychologists generally deny that a child can retain memories before turning three. But in my case the memory from my first year came clear in my mind when, one evening in 1943, Tony showed his home movies to our neighbors across the street.

In one scene, Tony was wheeling me in a perambulator down the street of a modest Hollywood working—class neighborhood. However, my personal recollection of lying in a pram on a sunny day was not created by the film; rather the film awakened an existing memory dating from my first year of life, giving me a vivid awareness of the blissful experience of lying in the pram, bathed in glorious sunlight.

Another vivid memory from before my third birthday was of a pedigreed dog that Tony had given to Boots at Christmas in 1941. The puppy, named "Bo-Jo," was a Bedlington Terrier, sired by a show dog named Bo-Jangles with Bo-Jeanne, also a show dog. I remember one day when Boots called Bo-Jo to come indoors from the front yard. She said that he was always getting cockle burrs in his dense fur, and she wanted to give him a bath. To this memory of my mother washing Bo-Jo in the bathtub was linked another memory, that of a bath she gave me. She had me stand in the tub, facing away from her (she had a puritanical streak, due to her Baptist upbringing). She washed my posterior and then moved her hand to wash my front, and I let out a loud giggle, saying, "That tickles!", and the bath ended.

Soon afterwards, Bo-Jo vanished. My mother told me that she hoped that whoever took Bo-Jo away from us was caring for him and feeding him well. I thought he might have been run over by a car, but my mother insisted that he was simply living with another family.

In 1943, still a few weeks before my third birthday, we moved to a large house on Broadlawn Drive, at walking distance from Universal Studios. The former owner of the house was a director who had used it as a *pied-à-terre* while shooting films. A live-in maid and cook kept the house in good order and prepared meals for him and his colleagues. The maid was there on the day we moved in. I asked her, "Now where are you going to live?" She answered, smiling, "In another part of town." And to keep me from asking any more questions, Tony spoke up and changed the subject.

Chapter 3

Boots immediately hired an African American cook and housekeeper, whose name was Cecilia, born of a family of self-liberated slaves who before the Civil War had fled from the slave states to California, where they found freedom and honest work. Formerly enslaved men were often hired to run cattle. In fact, contrary to the all-white Western movie stereotype of cowboys, one-fourth of the real cowboys riding the range were Black.

My father was somewhat racist, however, and used the excuse of Cecilia's breaking some drinking glasses to justify his firing her. Then he hired another cook and housekeeper. Her name was Marybelle: she was a Jehovah's Witness and an amateur pianist who performed a salon arrangement of the *Fourth*

Liebestraum of Liszt. One day she played it on my mother's Schuman baby grand piano, and the music immediately imprinted itself upon my mind. After Marybelle's performance I walked away humming the melody. Marybelle told me that *"Liebestraum"* was German for "a dream of love." I asked her to play it again, and she did so, several times.

When we had settled into our new home, my parents introduced themselves to our neighbors. Directly across from us were the Scoffields, who had two daughters: Diane, ten years old, and Elaine, seven, both of whom were taking piano lessons. Uphill from us was a gentleman from Northern Ireland, George O'Neill, with his English wife and their twelve-year-old daughter, Doreen. Mrs. O'Neill had been a swimming champion, having crossed the English Channel in both directions. One day Doreen asked me to come and meet her mother, explaining that she was ill. Doreen led me upstairs to her mother's room; she went to her mother's bedside and kissed her on the cheek, while I remained in the doorway. But Mrs. O'Neill said, "Don't be shy, darling—come in." She was very thin, but her smile was angelic.

Perhaps a week or two later, Doreen came to our house and asked my mother if she would cut some of our gorgeous red roses for her mother, who was leaving. Boots arranged the roses into a bouquet, and kept one rose for me, so that I could offer it to Mrs. O'Neill. Mr. O'Neill drove his car down the hill and pulled up to the curb by our house, so that his wife could say goodbye to their daughter. She kissed Doreen, who handed her the bouquet. Then I offered my rose and asked her, "Where are you going?"

She answered, "I'm going to the hospital, dear."

I felt prompted to ask, "And then where are you going?"

She said, "I'm going to heaven."

I asked her, "Where is that?"

She said, "That's where Jesus and the angels are."

I remember to this day the radiance of Mrs. O'Neill's smile and the peaceful tone of her voice as she said these words. Thus, I learned about the finality of death, and also about the ultimate hope: heaven and the beatific vision of God. From then on, I regarded Doreen as my special girlfriend, but I think she saw herself as a kind of teacher, especially in matters of religion, about which my parents avoided speaking.

My parents' silence about religion revealed a spiritual wound which both had suffered on account of their upbringings. Boots was a Southern Baptist, taught by her father, Arthur Francis Agee, who had been a preacher. Tony was a Polish boy and had been instructed in the Catholic faith by Irish priests. But Tony's mother exemplified another sort of Catholicism, which was of course quite Polish: in her bedroom she had a prayer corner with a crucifix and an image of the Blessed Virgin, together with photos of her grandchildren. And she went to confession faithfully, once a year.

On the doorstep of our home, Doreen, my mother, and I once had a conversation about the difference between a trip and a journey. "Are they different, because a journey is longer than a trip?" I asked. Doreen answered, "In the Bible there are stories about Abraham and his years of traveling to the promised land—that was a real, long journey!" A year or two later, I was with my mother on a weekend visit to a friend of hers who lived near Palm Springs, and my mother wanted to see the famous desert resort. So, she entrusted me to the care of a Sunday school teacher at a nearby Episcopal church. The lesson that Sunday was about Abraham as a young man obedient to God, who had called him to journey far from his home and family. The teacher showed us a reproduction of a painting of Abraham. This Sunday school lesson made me realize that I also wanted to make a long journey one day. And that my religion had to be a personal choice—in this, of course, I was whole-heartedly encouraged by both Boots and Tony.

Chapter 4

Another neighbor on Broadlawn Drive was Wenda Brainerd, who Monday through Friday walked to the Universal Motion-Picture Studios close by, where she worked in the costume department. Wenda had acted in silent films, but with the advent of talkies, she didn't feel herself capable of voice acting, so she chose to stay in the movie industry as a tailor, sewing and fitting costumes. Every Saturday evening, she invited actors and studio personnel to a party in her home, where her son Max, an electronics genius, would put on shows or record the guests' voices. Max had just turned twenty, and he already had two patented inventions to his credit. One of them was the "Flame Organ," a device that translated an audible sound recording into electrical signals that made fluorescent tubes, hidden behind a semi-transparent glass panel, flicker in a variety of colors—like flames—according to the music's rhythms and alternating pitches. Max's invention was one of the first electronic devices dedicated to multi-media home entertainment. Wenda was immensely proud of Max, her budding genius.

At one of Wenda's Saturday evening parties, I met a young movie star, Donald O'Conner. The memory of meeting him remained dormant for a few years, until my mother reminded me: "You remember, don't you, that you met Donald O'Conner at Wenda's?" Her words immediately triggered an image of Donald's presence in Wenda's home, sitting in a chair just inside the living-room door, and smoking a cigarette. He asks my name, and I tell him "Russell," and then I ask him one or two questions of my own. But what later emerged was a sense of his being somehow a friend. Years later, this vague sense of familiarity continued in the back of my mind as I watched him perform on the big screen or on television.

Every so often, movie people joined us for dinner at our own home. One was a character actor content with minor roles, and in his old age he was also seen on television. I have met other actors who have no interest in starring roles, and many of them are quite happy with briefly sharing the screen with the lead actors.

Chapter 5

Having reached the age of four, when parents in California could sign up their children for kindergarten, I wanted to begin first grade, I told my mother, "so that I can read books and learn arithmetic." Boots tried to enroll me in first grade at a private elementary school, but the principal of the school informed my mother that by law her son had to begin with kindergarten. When I broke out in tears, one of the teachers promised us that she would give me free piano lessons after school. So, I quickly learned to read notes, and after a few months I mastered the easy pieces in a textbook entitled *Teaching Little Fingers to Play.*

My parents were always glad to take me to the movies, although they were careful in choosing films; we usually attended the double-feature Saturday matinee, considered wholesome family entertainment. I understood films in general as a musical genre, and I listened to films as much as I watched them. I gradually came to realize that the spoken dialogue was never sufficient by itself to convey the full meaning of the words spoken on screen, and so I became accustomed, whenever I went to see a movie, to listen attentively, not only to the music, but also to sound effects, nature sounds, and the tone of voice with which actors delivered their lines.

Film music seemed to speak to me personally. I enjoyed musicals in which much of the dialogue was sung or expressed by dance, but I also appreciated dramatic films, with their sound effects and background music that emphasized and enhanced the spoken dialogue and the on-screen action. And it goes without saying that I enjoyed all the Disney films, short and long, and the delightful music that accompanied them.

Jackie Cooper, a young man who had become famous as a child actor, came to Tony's store many times. Seeing a photo-portrait of me in the show window—I was wearing a dark, formal suit and tie, but with short pants—Cooper gave my father a word of advice: "Chief" (Cooper always addressed Tony with this title), "don't let your son get roped into performing in movies!" Tony and Boots took his advice to heart. I'm glad they did.

However, Jackie Cooper did remain in the film industry, sometimes as a director. After two brief marriages, Cooper enjoyed fifty-four happy years with his third wife, Barbara Rae Kraus. They named their first child "Russell," but I have no way of knowing whether Cooper was thinking of the four-year-old in formal suit and tie, whom he had seen in the show window of the Matus Camera Supply Company. Then again, maybe he was thinking of me.

My own desire to know and understand this world I was living in led me to the realization that learning was more than just going to school. At a very early age I started reading newspapers, beginning with the headlines, but on Sundays Tony enjoyed seating me in his lap and reading the comics to me, so I hid my precocious ability to understand the printed word. He finally realized I could read when I pointed out to him a cartoon of a man who seemed drunk and had an arrow in his stomach; the caption, which I read out loud, was: "Intoxicated=shot with a poisoned arrow." I was not consciously trying to tell Tony to stop drinking, but in fact this was what I wanted him to do. Even at that young age, I sensed it was not good for my parents' marriage. Boots was not physically addicted to alcohol, even though she was psychologically co—dependent with Tony. I remember her words when he wanted to pour her another drink: "I've had enough, Tony." He did not insist, but he did refill his own glass.

At that moment the Second World War was raging: Britain was being bombed, and then President Franklin Delano Roosevelt died—I vividly remember the newsreel of this event, narrated over a somber portrait of the deceased president, followed by a scene of his successor, Harry S Truman, conversing with allies and advisors. I was worried: Truman, I thought, could never achieve the stature of Franklin D. Roosevelt, whom I had imagined was immortal (some others also thought so). Then a few Saturdays later, the newsreel showed the "mushroom cloud," the atomic bombing of Hiroshima and Nagasaki, filmed from the bomber itself. Never in my brief life had I felt so horrified. I sat there trembling, as the mushroom cloud expanded and seemed about to envelop the entire planet. Surely, I was not the only five-year-old whose sense of the future was defined by phrases like "world war" and "the atomic age."

In the face of this global death-threat, my only comfort was the hope that Liszt's "Dream of Love" and other melodies that accompanied movies might quiet the anxieties of little music-lovers like me, for whom life and music were inseparable: if I live, I'll make music; if I make music, I'll live.

Chapter 6

In 1945, just after my fifth birthday, Boots was diagnosed with tuberculosis in one of her lungs. Her doctor was an osteopathic physician whose name was Philip Morris (by coincidence, also the name of Boots' preferred brand of cigarettes). Dr. Morris earnestly recommended that she move to southern Arizona, near the city of Tucson [TOO-sahn], where she could receive/pneumothorax treatment as an out-patient. Boots told Tony that she needed the care that Dr. Morris suggested, which was available only in Arizona. Tony asked if she wanted to take their son with her. Her answer was clear: all three of us should go to Tucson, and she and Tony would raise their son together. Tony insisted on his staying in Hollywood and attending to the camera store, traveling back and forth to be with us. This was unacceptable to Boots; in the end her will prevailed. Tony sold the store, and we moved to Tucson.

Tony purchased four acres of land in the foothills of the Santa Catalina mountains and hired an architect, who quickly prepared the plans for a comfortable home in rustic Mexican—mission style, with a large fireplace in the living room and a picture· window in the dining room, looking south toward the city, whose evening lights we enjoyed seeing at dinner. During the construction of the house, Tony was always there, working alongside the skilled laborers, building the walls with burnt-adobe bricks imported from Mexico (the bricks had occupied an entire train car). In the meantime, we lived in a rented house near the center of town, and when our Catalina Foothills house was barely habitable, we immediately moved in.

While we were still in the rented house, Tony's parents came to visit us. I had no memory of meeting them before, and so I was fascinated by them, by their Polish accent and their fondness for my mother. They had been living In Canonsburg, Pennsylvania, where Tony and his siblings had received their first Holy Communion., And then the family moved to Denver, where a younger sister of my grandfather lived with her American husband. My grandparents did not stay long, since they were planning to settle in southern California, in the rural township of Bellflower; there I would see them again in the late nineteen-forties.

Life in the Arizona desert north of Tucson offered me and my parents a new experience of relating with nature. The desert surrounding us seemed exotic and wholly other than the landscapes any of us had known before. To the north we contemplated the Santa Catalina Mountains, the only major east-to-west range in North America. The flora seemed to have been transplanted from another planet, and the saguaro [sah-WAH-roh], a tree—sized cactus with upward-branching arms, dominated the panorama in every direction. Boots and Tony warned me not to wander too far and to keep the house always in sight, so I usually followed a dry creek bed down to the northwestern corner of our four acres, where I contemplated the largest saguaro ever seen, holding up its arms—more than fifty of them.

The climate was normally hot and dry, but now and then we would be visited with sudden showers, offering pleasant though brief interruptions of the dry heat. At night the temperature would sometimes plummet almost to freezing, returning to dry desert temperatures by midmorning. We also experienced the "monsoon season" of cloudbursts, followed by the glorious blossoming of what seemed like extra-terrestrial flowers on the saguaros and ocotillos and thorny shrubs, as if it were a sudden and evanescent spring. During our four winters in these high desert foothills, we experienced only one all-night snowfall, from which my mother gathered two cups of snow, and having flavored them with heavy cream, sugar and vanilla, she offered me this "snow cream" as a special breakfast treat.

Chapter 7

I had begun elementary school in downtown Tucson and completed first grade. In the foothills I would attend grades two and three at the nearby public school. The Catalina Foothills School had two large classrooms—Mrs. Chumbly's room for grades one through three and Miss Connor's for grades four through eight. In September 1947, I was beginning second grade. Mrs. Chumbly told the children to transcribe into longhand the sentences that she had written in block letters on the blackboard. I raised my hand and told her that at the school in town we were not taught longhand. She replied, a bit sternly, "Well, you are going to learn longhand right now!"

The exercise I turned in was partly in imitation of my father's standard longhand and partly imitating my mother's exotic backhand. Mrs. Chumbly was pleased with my first calligraphic exercise.

Tony sent an invitation to his siblings—most were living in Long Beach, south of Los Angeles—to come and see the new house and the splendid desert. Helen came with her second husband, Ford Andrews, and Virginia with her second or third, Willard Lee. They were with us for one night, and then they went to see the Grand Canyon. The two sisters asked Tony, "Why don't you send your son to spend a week with us and his grandparents in Long Beach, and then we'll put him on a plane so he can fly back to Tucson?" Boots was worried, but Helen assured her that there had never been any passenger plane crashes in Southern California. I was enthusiastic and enjoyed my grandparents, whose conversations in Polish fascinated me.

Upon arriving at Uncle Ford's and Aunt Helen's home, I found the Tuesday morning edition of the newspaper, the *Los Angeles Examiner,* July 8, 1947, which had a front-page article about the crash of a flying saucer near the town of Roswell in New Mexico. The article—dated just two days after the reported crash—was not from any news service, but from an unnamed military source. In other newspapers the articles about the Roswell event came a day later, quoting military officers who denied all talk of extraterrestrials and claimed that the crash debris was from weather balloons. Years later, military sources claimed that the debris was from life-sized dummies (unknown in 1947) used for testing the effects of bailing out of planes. Few have ever believed the official explanations, especially when they were mutually incompatible. After sundown on my first day with Aunt Helen, I saw lights reflecting off the clouds, and with just a little fear I asked her, "Aunt Helen, are those lights from flying saucers?" She answered, "No, darling; there must be a new movie in town, and they project those lights to make people come and watch the film."

On the next morning with Aunt Helen, I found a bi-weekly magazine with an article on the various ways the world might end. Hyper-realistic images by the artist Chesley Bonestell accompanied the article. One of the images suggested the effect of a "dwarf star" (technical term: "micro-stellar object") that comes close to our planet and would pull up objects, animals and humans. I asked Uncle Ford, "Where will those people go?" He answered, "Certainly they would land on some other world." And he continued reading his newspaper. But I was used to non-answers from adults. Likewise, I never heard a response from anyone about Mrs. O'Neill's expressing her faith that she would be with Jesus and his angels. She believed it and made me ready to believe it myself.

After a couple more days, Aunt Virginia brought me to the airport for the American Airlines flight to Tucson. I was to fly in an impressive four-engine plane, and as I went to board the plane she said, "Remember to tell them you are eight years old!" I said, "Don't worry, Aunt Virginia. That's my Chinese age—I'll remember."

Aboard the big plane in full flight, my eyes were glued to the window. I was fascinated with the minutiae on the ground: towns and croplands, mountains and sandy deserts. I arrived in Tucson early that afternoon, and my parents were there to meet me. Tony said, "You're a big boy, now! Come and sit in the front seat with your mother and me on the way home."

Chapter 8

In Arizona, we regularly attended the double-feature Saturday matinee. I enjoyed Broadway-style musicals, in which much of the dialogue was sung and underlined by dance, culminating with what today many movie commentators consider the greatest of them all: *Singin' in the Rain,* with Gene Kelly, Debbie Reynolds and Donald O'Conner (again, my mother reminded me that I had met O'Conner at one of Wenda's parties). I also appreciated dramatic films, with their sound effects and background music that emphasized and enhanced the spoken dialogue and the tense action on the screen. I began listening to films as much as I watched them, and I gradually came to realize that spoken dialogue was never sufficient to convey the full meaning of what happened on-screen. Films began to speak to me personally, often in the language of music. So, I strove to listen attentively to the musical score, and to sound effects, nature sounds, and the tone of voice with which actors delivered their lines.

It was a beautiful spring day in 1948, when my parents suffered, practically without injury, an automobile accident as they were driving down from the foothills. They had planned to pick me up as soon as school was out—at about 2 p.m.—to take me to the Ringling Brothers' Circus. I was standing in front of the school, waiting for my father's car. Almost an hour passed, and I started to cry. A cleaning lady brought me an ice cream cone and said, "Don't worry, child, your parents will be here soon."

In fact, I had just finished the ice cream when a car pulled over into the school parking area. But it was not my father's Chrysler. Boots got out of the car and ran over to me, and said, "Darling, we had an accident, but your father and I are all right." (I noticed that she had a neat bandage on the right side of her forehead.) The driver of the car was a doctor, who had driven by the scene of their accident, and seeing my parents outside the car, he had turned back and pulled over. Seeing blood trickling down Boots' forehead, he went to get his doctor's valise from his car. He treated and bandaged her wound, which was only superficial, and then asked Tony if he were all right. He said he was, and thanked the doctor, asking him also to do us the favor of taking us to our home, since our car could not function. And then he told the doctor the whole story. "We were on our way to take our son to the circus, but all of a sudden I could no longer steer the car—the previous week another car had rammed us from the side, but I didn't notice any serious damage, and I didn't have it checked out at the garage. Now I realize that the axle broke, on account of last week's accident. Could you please take us home? It's just north of here."

We arrived home, and the doctor told my mother that he would be staying at the hotel in downtown Tucson, so that if she came, he could take another look at her injury. Boots and Tony thanked him, and my mother said she would spend the rest of the day in bed and see him in the morning. Since Tony also had a truck, he could use it to take Boots to see the doctor. When Boots met with him, the doctor found no signs of concussion or skull fracture. Then Tony got an automobile repair shop to go up to the foothills and bring the car back down. The automotive and structural damages were repaired. Tony could not afford a paint job, but the car was fit for the road, and it would bring us back to California. In the meantime, work on our Catalina Foothills home was reaching completion, and then Tony would put it on the real-estate market.

A final word about Mrs. Chumbly, our teacher at the Catalina Foothills school—my one public school teacher whom I remember well and whom I missed. She had recognized precocious intellectual gifts in me and my good ear for music. The school where she taught was part of the Arizona public school system, but you could almost see it as a private school, supported as it was by wealthy families nearby, who provided the teachers with extra funds for purchasing books, movie projectors and long-play record players. Tony took a photo of our class, with Mrs. Chumbly; years later I noticed her Native American appearance. Most of the Indios in Arizona were

Catholics, so I thought that she might have been Catholic also.

I have a vivid memory of Mrs. Chumbly having us listen to Ferde Grofe's orchestral masterpiece, *Grand Canyon Suite*, as a lesson both in geography and in contemporary classical music. As usual, I retained note-for-note the principal melody of the movement called "On the Trail" and would sometimes sing it to myself. Then my parents went to the school to say goodbye to Mrs. Chumbly. I stood outside the door while they were speaking to her and thanking her, and then I heard Mrs. Chumbly crying.

Chapter 9

For a year now, Boots had been in remission from her tuberculosis. Still in the Catalina Foothills above Tucson, we celebrated Christmas in 1948. There were presents at the foot of the Christmas tree, including two wind-up mechanical toys for me. I didn't know what to do with them, but then I thought—or an inner voice spoke to me—of taking them apart, which I found interesting, with the challenge not only of sorting out the pieces but also of putting them back together again and getting them to run as before. Then I could sincerely thank my father for the gifts.

All three of us were happy when Boots' doctor told her that her tuberculosis had been in remission for more than a year. After Tony had found a buyer for our home in the foothills, both he and Boots spoke eagerly of returning to California. We started packing, and since we had both a dog (our outdoor pet) and a cat (our indoor pet), I was told to choose only one of them for the journey. My choice was for the cat, a male whose name.was Bushy or "Buszy" (meaning "kisses" in my grandmother's Polish dialect). When I took Buszy out into the garden to get him ready to leave, he ran to the fence—he must have suspected something unpleasant—but I caught him. I took the collar off the dog and put it on Buszy, so that, to the amazement of many, I could lead him on the leash whenever we parked the car. Tony's 1938 Chrysler sedan was still puissant, and so we left Tucson in May of 1949. We were heading east from Tucson—wrong way? No, Boots and Tony had decided to extend the trip to include the Grand Canyon, Mammoth Caves, my mother's relatives in Texas, and, in Colorado, Tony's daughter by his first marriage—her name was Arlyne, and like her mother Eudora, she attended Christian Science services.

The trip began with an excursion into northern Mexico just after leaving Tucson. There we visited a very old church, the first Catholic church I ever entered, and the priest who gave us a tour of the church was the first priest I ever met. First seeds in the soil of my soul! We enjoyed perfect weather during these three weeks, and our next destination was Fort Worth, Texas, my mother's birthplace.

I was fascinated by the Texas dialect of Boots' relatives, especially her aunts and uncles—fascinated also by the fact that Boots herself had completely lost the accent. As usual I listened to their words with my musical ear, and sometimes I imitated their phrases, though without intending to mock them. During our week in Texas, I realized there was in fact very little uniformity in American speech. In their youth, both my parents felt strongly motivated to speak perfect American English as heard on the radio or in movies, leaving no hint of either a Texan or a Polish accent.

My maternal grandfather, Arthur Francis Agee, owned a small farm in Arkansas, and he invited Boots and me to join him on an overnight trip there. The countryside was shrouded in dense fog, which only enhanced the remarkable beauty of the farmland. But the time had come for the three of us to go visit my half-sister Arlyne, who was living with her mother in Denver. She had spent a couple of weeks with us when we had just arrived in Tucson, so this was not the first time I saw her. Arlyne showed great affection for her father, who deeply loved both her and me. But however warm and gentle Boots was to her, Arlyne did not seem to feel that Boots and I were family. Decades would then pass, and when I once again met her, just after my ordination as a priest, Arlyne showed genuine affection toward me, saying that she was proud of her half brother and his ministry. She also became friendly with Boots and admired her intellectual gifts.

Chapter 10

Having visited relatives in various states, we turned westwards, and re-entering Arizona we stopped briefly to contemplate the Grand Canyon, the very sight of which gave me vertigo. After the third day, as we left Arizona, I began singing, "California, here I come, right back where I started from. . ." and my parents joined in. We would soon be living in San Bernardino, sixty miles (= 97 km) due east of Los Angeles.

I still thought of Hollywood as home, even though it is not a distinct city; rather, it is part of a broad urban environment within Los Angeles County, while also overlapping some of West Hollywood, including the Samuel Goldwyn Studios. So Hollywood was indeed urban, but with a difference:

the residential, commercial and movie—industry areas were mixed in with each other. The dimensions of Los Angeles initially gave rise to an excellent system of public transport, but public transportation suddenly disappeared after the inauguration of the first freeway, the Arroyo Seco, linking Pasadena with downtown L.A. The futuristic network of elevated urban highways expanded rapidly, because Angelinos clearly preferred their private vehicles to public transportation. Returning from Tucson, I saw Los Angeles becoming quite different from how my precocious childhood memories still imagined it to be.

By 1949 the Los Angeles smog had thickened, but it had not yet reached San Bernardino, which lay at the foot of a mountain range, close to desert land that seemed much like Tucson but without the saguaros. The usually warm, dry weather was perfect for my mother, who energetically joined Tony in creating a "Matus Furniture and Decorating Service," useful for our own home life but also necessary as a source of income. We took our own furniture out of storage to furnish the house that Tony had leased, especially the Schuman baby grand piano, my own twin beds, and the more-than-double bed that my parents had purchased when we moved into the house on Broadlawn Drive.

At home again in California, my parents continued their customary attendance at the Saturday matinee showing of new films, plus animated films for the little ones. I was "little" in the sense that I was still only nine, but I soon developed my own tastes in films and reading materials, and my mother's liberal streak inclined her to let me use my father's library card to check out books from the public library, no questions asked.

In the late 1940s San Bernardino was to all intents and purposes an agricultural town. Vast orange groves filled the fertile land to the south, but there were other farms as well, whose tax revenues enabled the city to sustain a rich cultural scene. San Bernardino boasts two women of fame in the arts: Edith Head, born in San Bernardino, was the greatest movie costume creator of the twentieth century and the only woman to be awarded eight Oscars. Twyla Tharp, an innovative choreographer famous for her "crossover ballet," was born in Indiana, but she was raised in San Bernardino, where she attended Pacific High School, from which I graduated a year before she did. When she began her college education at San Bernardino Valley College, I was a sophomore at Occidental College in Los Angeles.

My relationship with Boots and Tony was not like that of a typical American boy with his mom and dad. In fact, I had intentionally begun to imitate adult speech patterns, almost imagining that the three of us were of the same generation. After all, I thought, now that I had turned ten, my age was in double digits like theirs. I respected my mother's Baptist upbringing, so I was careful to avoid certain "bad" words and topics that might trouble or offend her.

Nonetheless, I was still in many ways a child, even while nurturing cultural interests to which few boys my age would have been attracted. I also began to observe girls, of my own age or older. This attraction to the opposite sex was not yet fully erotic, but it did provoke a subtle and delightful sense of lightness, like "walking on clouds".

Months later, on a train taking us back to Tucson, where Tony was to finalize the sale of the Catalina Foothills home, I became obsessed with a girl seated alongside her mother on the opposite side of the car and one row back. I pretended to be sleepy and leaned my head on the arm rest so that I could watch the pretty lass. She did not look in my direction, but her mother saw me and wisely offered me a home-baked cookie, which broke the spell.

Chapter 11

At the age of ten, on my own initiative I started to attend Sunday School at Calvary Baptist Church, a short walk from our house. One Sunday the head preacher at Calvary Baptist, Doctor Boyce van Osdell, spoke to our Sunday School class, inviting the boys and girls who would be eleven years of age by Easter Sunday, 1951, to receive Baptism. I signed up, and the following Lent, I attended classes on baptism and made my personal commitment to Jesus Christ as my Lord and Savior. I also saw the film *Quo Vadis,* based on a novel by Polish author Henryk Sienkiewicz, a devout Catholic, with its vision of first-century apostolic Christianity. During the Easter Sunday evening service, I and several classmates were baptized "in the name of the Father and of the

Son and of the Holy Ghost." My experience was that of living out, in my own day, the story of the film *Quo Vadis.*

In 1952, my mother gave me a copy of the *Autobiography of a Yogi,* by Paramhansa Yogananda, calling my attention to the section in which Yogananda outlines the basic principles of India's classical music. It occurred to me that the book had first been in the hands of my mother's sister Vera Lee (my Aunt Billee), who in recent years had expanded her spiritual horizons to embrace both Buddhism and neo-Marxist theories.

I did indeed take interest in Yogananda's brief but profound presentation of the "foundation stone of Hindu music…the *ragas* or fixed melodic scales." At that time I probably had never heard an authentic performance of India's classical music, but what drew me into this autobiography was the author's understanding of yoga, not as some sort of exotic calisthenics but as a vast cultural and mystical panorama, showing a way toward realizing the "Self," referring to the Sanskrit words *atman-brahman,* meaning (depending on context), "breath" or "spirit" or the

Absolute "one without a second." In other words, yoga does not begin from the ego expressing itself through the body but from the transcendent Divine Essence who is the source and ultimate end of every human soul.

Here was the truth I wanted to know by experience: the absolute immanence of God in all that exists, especially in each sentient being, and hence in myself. Then I turned to page one and began to read.

The discovery of India, of its yoga and of its music, somehow threaded itself through my life as a high school student and a piano student at the keyboard of my mother's baby grand piano. There was a potential synthesis here, and you will see it woven through the rest of this book.

Later in that same year, Boots was again diagnosed with active tuberculosis. The diagnosis was less troubling than the one in 1945, since in the meantime two new antibiotics—streptomycin and P.A.S.—were found quite effective in its treatment. Boots had to be hospitalized, and I was totally prohibited from visiting her. An exception was made for my thirteenth birthday in February of the following year. The treatment was declared a success, and her immunity lasted the rest of her life. My mother lived until 1990, and on the solemnity of the Transfiguration of Jesus, August 6, more than three months after her eightieth birthday, concluded an amazingly long life, considering her premature birth and her two bouts with TB.

In 1956, I changed my legal address in San Bernardino from Tony's furniture and decorating service to that of Boots' suburban apartment, just off a charming courtyard. My father had been unable to overcome his alcohol addiction, and my mother had made the painful decision we could no longer live in this situation. A civil court granted her a divorce, due to take effect the following June; as a minor I was to live with her. Another result of the divorce was that I now belonged to another school district and was obliged to attend San Bernardino's new high school in the Fall. The school was named "Pacific High," and was in a wealthier area of San Bernardino where many upper-class families had their homes. On account of the predominance of "A's" on my report cards, I was designated valedictorian for the graduation ceremony in June.

I regretted the fact that another top student had previously been designated to give the valedictory speech (he was popular among our classmates, while I was unknown), but fortunately the school named him to be "co-valedictorian," so that he too could give a speech. I wound up offering the concluding valedictory address, which I had composed in iambic pentameter so as to anchor my delivery in Shakespearean rhythm.

There was a certain affectation in this, for which I silently scolded myself, but ultimately, I delivered the speech as written. I received compliments from classmates and from my girlfriend, MaryAnn Kahl— blond like me and also a gifted linguist. When I visited her home, I was very much impressed when I saw above her desk a Latin motto: *Labor me vocat:* "Work is calling me." I asked her to be my date at the senior prom, and she eagerly said yes. But what was happening in the depths of my soul pointed in another direction, clearly away from marriage.

My eight years in San Bernardino led to a difficult but necessary examination of my human and religious identity. I wandered through all this self-examination, in some respects painful, but in the end, I was able to resolve at least some of my problems, especially after I had begun the Bachelor of Arts program at Occidental College. The demands of serious liberal-arts studies, along with a major in music composition, perhaps in view of becoming a composer of film scores—all this demanded an unwavering focus.

Chapter 12

As I approached my teens, an intense focus on classical music took the place of church attendance and Bible reading. I had two musician friends, Melvin Kinder and Delbert Riddle, both ahead of me in school and deep into contemporary classical music. I began listening to all the recordings of 20th-century music that I could borrow from the San Bernardino public library. Mel introduced me to Igor Stravinsky's *Rite of Spring*, which greatly expanded my musical horizons.

Then I checked out Bela Bartok's *Music for Strings, Percussion and Celesta*, recorded at a concert financed by the Maharaja of Mysore in India. I had no idea what kind of music to expect. Bartok's *"Music"* begins with a solemn fugue, based on a chromatic melody stated by the two choirs of violas in a very slow tempo. Hearing the first five notes of the fugue, I felt as if an electric shock had been applied to the base of my spine, transporting me through deep space from this world to a distant planet, whose atmosphere the theme evoked and where Bartok's music was being performed at an outdoor concert. I was instantly mesmerized, and I immediately perceived this masterpiece of Bartok as a possible accompaniment to a science fiction film, although I did not presume to imagine that I was the first person to have had this idea.

Every week I listened to a different record from the San Bernardino public library, often chosen purposely because I had no previous knowledge of the composer. Despite the fact I was no longer living with him, Tony was still my loving father and heartily encouraged my interest in music. More, he found ways of paying for private piano lessons, often by providing the teachers with free interior decorating services and by re upholstering their furniture. Every few months I had a new piano teacher, until, just before my fourteenth birthday, I was accepted as a student by Howard Lindholm, then a highly regarded teacher in his native San Bernardino.

During his teens in Paris, Lindholm had been trained as a concert pianist and later, at the University of Southern California, he had been a student of Arnold Schoenberg. Drafted into the army and taken captive as a wounded prisoner of war in Korea, he was no longer able to pursue his ambition to perform twentieth-century piano masterpieces in public, so he dedicated himself to the musical education of children.

He and I both realized that I was not spending sufficient time practicing at home, but he recognized my need to make sure my high school grades would earn me scholarships and guarantee my admission to Occidental College, from which I would graduate in June of 1961, *magna cum laude,* at the head of the music department's graduating class.

Before my freshman year at Oxy, however, I subscribed to the correspondence course in yoga and meditation offered by Yogananda's Self-Realization Fellowship. My senior year of high school had demanded my hitting the books and burning the midnight oil, but I accepted this as basic training for my college studies, as well as for my immersion into every book about Yoga, Hinduism and Buddhism that I could find in the public and college libraries. And, of course, I re-read the *Autobiography of a Yogi* slowly and meditatively.

During my first three years of college, I did not attend the Sunday services on campus but rather the services and meditations at Yogananda's Hollywood temple, and after my first year as a devotee, I was initiated into Kriya Yoga, the meditation practice of the legendary Himalayan forest-dweller Babaji [BAH-buh-gee], as transmitted by his chosen disciple Lahiri Mahasaya, a brahmin. It was precisely by following this path—a path of silent devotion, transcending the senses, mind and intellect—that I ultimately discovered the Catholic mystics.

Reading some of their life stories, I realized that their spirituality was nourished by the Church's creeds and sacraments which the mystics embraced, together with their devout reading of the Bible. Thus, the idea of this Christian mystical lineage had already presented itself to me before my actual conversion to the Catholic faith and to the Church's understanding of mystical union with God by faith through grace and by means of the Church's sacraments.

Chapter 13

At the time, however, I more strongly identified myself with the young Yogananda, then known as Mukunda. After Mukunda had found his guru, Swami Sriyukteshwar, and only after graduating from Serampore College out of obedience to both his guru and his father, he was given the name Yogananda and was clothed in saffron robes (the saffron or orange color is a sign of a swami's renunciation of worldly goods and family life). And by then I knew enough about myself to realize that I, personally, could not virtuously practice Kriya Yoga unless I had also renounced the ownership of property and an active sex life (even though I had been taught by devotees of Yogananda that both were good). In other words, I was orienting my not-yet-Catholic mind toward some basic principles that would lead me in the direction of Saint Anthony, one of the first Christian desert elders of Egypt, and of Saint Benedict and other monastic saints whom the Catholic Church venerates.

I knew little about Catholic religious consecration, but I took it for granted that Christian monastic vows were equivalent to a swami's renunciation, the shaving of his head and his being clothed in a saffron/orange robe. This supposition was re-enforced by a book called *Seeds of Contemplation,* whose author was Thomas Merton, himself a Christian monk. I was amazed to find these words in his Preface: "Above all, remember that in this book the author is talking about spiritual things from the point of view of experience rather than in the concise terms of dogmatic theology or of metaphysics. In religion, as in the natural life, the language of experience and the language of dogma or science may find themselves opposed." I thought: "Paramhansa Yogananda could not have said it better!"

I felt that I had indeed learned something about what goes on in a monk's mind from reading Yogananda's *Autobiography:* "a great novel" as one of his Hindu friends called it with a touch of sarcasm. The two autobiographies—Merton's *Seven Storey Mountain* in 1942, Yogananda's *Autobiography* in 1946—were published only four years apart and were best-sellers in their respective genres. Fortunately, I did not begin with Merton's best-seller, but rather with his later, and more serene, *The Sign of Jonas.* It has occurred to me that, had I read only Merton's *Seven Storey Mountain* and nothing else of his, I might never have become a Catholic. Let me explain this, by comparing the respective opening paragraphs of Merton and Yogananda.

From Merton's *Seven Storey Mountain:* "On the last day of January 1915, under the sign of the Water Bearer, in a year of a great war, and down in the shadow of some French mountains on the border of Spain, I came into the world. Free by nature, in the image of God, I was nevertheless the prisoner of my own violence and my own selfishness, in the image of the world into which I was born. That world was the picture of Hell, full of men [sic] like myself, loving God and yet hating Him; born to love Him, living instead in fear and hopeless self-contradictory hungers."

From Yogananda's *Autobiography of a Yogi:* "The characteristic features of Indian culture have long been a search for ultimate verities and the concomitant disciple/guru relationship. My own path led me to a Christlike sage whose beautiful life was chiseled for the ages. He was one of the great masters who are India's sole remaining wealth. Emerging in every generation, they have bulwarked their land against the fate of Babylon and Egypt." Yogananda's first sentence gave me two new words: "verities" and "concomitant". Merton's third sentence opened with his desolating assertion: "That world was the picture of Hell. …"

The Sign of Jonas, Merton's second autobiography, went to press in 1953, eleven years after The *Seven Storey Mountain.* I have often wondered if readers of his first book ever questioned the author's harsh judgments regarding the world he lived in, judgments that he also seemed to be hurling at non-monastics and persons of other faiths. But I suspected that a man as sincere as Merton would revisit those earlier judgments, which he did in his second memoir.

I do understand why Merton, as a self-accused "prisoner of his own violence and his own selfishness," needed to do battle against a nature fallen away from its own primordial image: God. But in my opinion, the better philosophical presuppositions were those of Yogananda. The latter's Hindu guru, Swami Sriyukteshwar, was "Christlike" and his "beautiful life" had been "chiseled for the ages"—here, the passive voice of the participle "chiseled," as in similar Bible passages, is a statement of God's hidden activity, in this case as sculptor of the soul. Merton had been validly baptized at birth as an Anglican, but as a Catholic convert, on the contrary, he believed that he had been born a prisoner in a world that was the image of hell. So, I had to conclude that Merton, in his first autobiography, failed to show us much Christian hope, whereas Yogananda gave voice to the primeval hope expressed in the Hindu chant to the Absolute, invoked as "God the beautiful," *Sundaradeva.*

Chapter 14

God's first grace in my journey toward Catholic faith was the paragraph in *The Sign of Jonas* which occupies a page just after the ecclesiastical approval, *imprimatur.* Merton's says, "The sign Jesus promised to the generation that did not understand him was the 'sign of Jonas the prophet'... that is, the sign of His own resurrection. The life of every monk, of every priest, of every Christian is signed with the sign of Jonas, because we all live by the power of Christ's resurrection. But I feel that my own life is especially sealed with this great sign, which baptism and monastic profession and priestly ordination have burned into the roots of my being, because like Jonas himself I find myself traveling toward my destiny in the belly of a paradox."

As I was just beginning my freshman year at Occidental College, my mother left San Bernardino for Honolulu. It was in this context that my mother decided to return to the use of her baptismal name "Clara," instead of her teen-age nickname "Boots." She had spent a few months on O'ahu with a married couple who were her best friends: Ruth and Chuck Small. Ruth was a piano teacher and a concert accompanist. Clara remained' enchanted with the Islands, not only for their tropical-oceanic environment, but above all for the multi-racial population as it related to the campaign for statehood. Alaska had just become the forty-ninth state, thanks to the collaborative efforts of the governor of Alaska and the governor of the territory of Hawaii. Both governors had for many years been close friends, despite their different political persuasions (the Alaskan was a Republican and the Hawai'ian was a Democrat). But together they were able to convince absolute majorities in Congress to favor the statehood of both territories. Historians of the United States may ultimately count the incorporation of Alaska and Hawaii among the greatest events of our country's history.

During my high school years, Clara had been employed by the San Bernardino Public Schools. She had acquired top skills in computer programming and contributed to a service that would coordinate many aspects of the educational programs in all the grades. She spent her summers taking courses at the IBM computer headquarters in Los Angeles, and several of the IBM staff suggested that she make computers in Hawaii's public schools a personal project. So, with her skills having been recognized by IBM and the public-school systems, she moved permanently to Hawari, initially staying with Ruth and Chuck on the windward side of O'ahu and beginning a computer education program in a private business school across the street from the Catholic cathedral.

Clara invited me to spend my summer vacations with her, and of course I was delighted with the interfaith exchanges in the schools, not only among Christians but also with the various Buddhist temples, that served almost a third of the State population. Not having the means to travel in Asia, I was happy to be immersed in an environment where

Buddhist meditation was taught and was a valued spiritual practice for many non-Buddhists as well.

My intensely focused senior year at Pacific High School in San Bernardino had earned me two scholarships to Occidental College. By God's grace I maintained sufficiently high marks during my first year at Oxy to keep them. I worked particularly hard in my music major, specializing in the composition techniques of twentieth-century classical composers, especially Bela Bartok, Arnold Schoenberg and Anton Webern. My composition mentor was Professor Robert Gross, a brilliant concert violinist, widely known for having premiered many important avant-garde works for violin solo, chamber ensembles, and concerti. But something kept drawing me away from music: the daily practice of meditation according to Yogananda 's Kriya Yoga.

Chapter 15

As I approached the end of my first academic year, I began to nurture the idea that to "realize God" as a yogi, I had to eliminate distractions from my mind, especially those of scholastic achievement and even classical music—although I thought that chanting according to Indian *ragas* would not be that kind of distraction.

Soon, I had fully accepted the notion that divine grace and divine wisdom were flowing into me from Yogananda's teachings, and I was ready to apply for admission as a resident monastic at either Yogananda's Los Angeles mother-house on Mount Washington or at his Hollywood temple. If I were accepted, I would have to renounce my scholarships. I shared this idea with my mother, and she calmly entreated me to think again and not to do anything abrupt. Her suggestion was that I should speak with Brahmachari Leland (named Brother Bhaktananda after his solemn vows); better yet, that she should accompany me to Mount Washington.

Leland was cheerful and gentle; he welcomed my mother and showed respect for her and also for my novice fervor. But he convinced me with the story of another young college genius, Donald Walters, an SRF monastic brother with the name Kriyananda, who at the end of his senior year at college decided to forego the final examinations, got into his car, and drove cross country to Los Angeles. When Donald presented himself to Master Yogananda, the Master moaned, and raising his eyes to heaven he said, "Why does Divine Mother do these things to me?" In other words, Donald was convinced that the Mother knew his spiritual needs, and that the cross—country drive would do him better than any advice from his parents; so, the Master accepted him.

Since I knew myself and those who loved me, I realized that my abandoning a college education would not be an expression of religious devotion, but a hurtful act of ingratitude toward the two persons who loved me most—Clara and Tony. So that settled the issue, and both Brahmachari Leland and Clara were relieved and grateful.

At this point in the narration of my life as meditator and monk, I need to step back and let my soul speak for itself—but what language does the soul speak? Not that I lack courage to face the truth and tell it. I began this diary with the desire to put in writing the state of my soul, but I am still not sure I know how to do so. Not that I am reluctant to face my inner state and make it known to my readers, but I also desire that my telling be clear and expressed in the language proper to the soul, with its own secret eloquence. I think that, if I succeed in writing in my soul's language, I could reach other souls and be understood. And if I succeed in expressing my struggle with what is not yet in my soul, I could truthfully speak of what is there now.

Ought I to be cautious at the self-confidence I feel? I want to pray in the language of silence, but the words come to me as a question: "Is my habit of immediately turning my thoughts to God upon awakening an obsessive-compulsive behavior?" I answer my own question: "No," because prayer of any kind is already a state of union with God, since it is God's own Spirit who prays in us "with sighs too deep for words," as Saint Paul put it. Anyone's prayer is an expression of serene friendship with the One who loves every praying soul and gives her permission to pray when and as she wants, so that the soul might ask for whatever good she wants, being sure of God's offer of forgiveness for any and all sins.

Chapter 16

I have something else to write about: first, on the thought of myself as a child of God in and through Jesus the only begotten of God, who was also the first of the many children of Mary the ever-virgin Mother. All Mary's children were born from their respective birth mothers to receive the grace of God and the gift of faith, through her intercession. I learned to join in my sweet grandmother Wladyslawa's prayer: "I talk to dear God." In this moment of my journey of faith, I want to surrender myself to God in my gratefulness.

I accept my condition as a human, a creature, endowed with a certain foundation slowly built by the laying of psychological and cultural bricks over many years and decades. I accept the state of a male human born of a female. I accept *Gabe und Aufgabe,* the task born of a gift, for which I give thanks; nature that urges me to give what I have and what I am, and to transform all that I am into culture. Yes, we are all born free—see again the evidence of perinatal memories gathered by Stanislaw Grof and others. We are all free by nature, and our freedom is formed by our birth culture, but no less by the culture we give birth to: this begins with what is given unto us, what lies within us, and what we do with the initial gift.

My personal liberty is both a gift of nature and a gift of the divine Author of my human nature. My culture is also a space in which I move, and hence it both enables and defines my movement. For example, Catholicism is my inheritance, although I came into this inheritance after two decades of living without it. There have also been the many teachers who walked with me along the way: my parents, Mrs. Chumbly, Dr. van Osdell, Yogananda—did they not lay the groundwork for me? Were not the years of near-total immersion in Kriya Yoga and Yogananda's way of meditating a foundation for what came later?

One affirmation that the Church gave me is the affirmation of nature, intrinsically good and never a direct occasion for sin: *Naturalia non sunt turpia.* Can a culture be or become intrinsically evil? What can be said about the culture of Fascism and Nazism, especially keeping in mind their infiltration into certain sectors of the Roman Church, even among illustrious theologians and monks? Surely, this was a serious challenge to society in general and to the Church itself. And what about the military-industrial complex, in view of its commercial links with the sale of arms and drugs? And what can we say about the medical culture that promotes abortion as a legitimate means for birth control, thus contradicting the Hippocratic Oath? And at the root of today's culture, what can be said about the mechanistic paradigm of the human body itself? Where does culture end and the abuse of freedom begin? Is today's culture in general pushing humankind toward a perverted worldview?

It is a historical fact that the mechanistic paradigm of the human body and of the universe still maintains its prevailing influence, even in philosophical and religious thought. In view of the fact that the progressive wing of European politics has generally embraced the democratic system, a new danger has arisen from certain nostalgic political movements: will these become a rehash of Fascism? We Americans need to keep our eyes open to signs of political nostalgia and take seriously the risk of populist and authoritarian influences even within traditional political entities.

In my early teens I had begun a free reading of the Bible. Having discovered the Psalms, I began reading them as poetry—which in fact they are. I was particularly fascinated by the longest of the 150 Psalms, number 119 (or 118 for Catholics). I said to myself, "One day I want to set that psalm to music." Twenty years later I did, based on the Italian version of the Psalms, while encouraging others to contribute melodies for our daily prayer. This work was published as *Salterio monastico, canto e preghiera (Monastic Psalter, Song and Prayer)*. It provides all the musical settings needed for the celebration of the Liturgy of the Hours, plus settings suitable also for the Mass and other liturgical celebrations.

Chapter 17

Going back to my pre-teens and early teens, I have vague memories of how my classmates tried to make me loosen up so that I could join in their fun and games. I was proud and stubborn (still am to a lesser degree), but underneath there was an undefinable fear, and sometimes I used religion as an excuse for my refusal to be drawn in to the group. The consequence was solitude, made deeper by what was indeed a truly religious need. I was sure that boys and girls of my age were incapable of feeling what I felt—I was not totally wrong in this—and much less were they capable, as I thought I was, of enduring what I endured.

I became an avid reader of science fiction, and I consoled myself with fantasies that were sometimes obviously absurd but also efficacious in escaping the miseries of my parents, for whom I kept alive a heartfelt love, as a sincere response to their unconditional love of their son. And then there was always schoolwork: exams, term papers, books to read and to report on. I was the straight-A student, always at the head of the class, a fact that set me apart but also attracted esteem from classmates, despite my deliberate distancing from their company.

Still, I was mostly alone. I sought consolation in imagining myself as an extraterrestrial, an alien, a mutant. Serious sci-fi literature gave me images and words for explaining my own secret self to myself. I was convinced that no one could join me in the place to which I had come on my own. If at times I tried to imagine another path I might follow, back then it was not a Catholic hermitage. But I also had sights set on a spiritual denouement for my story, and for three years this longing was addressed at the Self-Realization Fellowship, whose Mount Washington Center was a brisk half-hour walk from Occidental College.

But music was still a crucial part of my life. A high point during my junior year at Oxy was Professor

Robert Grass's performance of Aram Khatchaturian's violin concerto with the Los Angeles Philharmonic Orchestra, the first performance west of the Rockies of this 20th-century masterpiece. That same year the Occidental music and drama departments joined in producing Stravinsky's *Histoire du soldat* ("A Soldier's Tale"), exactly as desired by Stravinsky for its premier performance. The composer had of course been invited, but he sent a message of apology, explaining that his doctor would not permit him to leave his bed. During my senior year Professor Gross gave a solo violin recital entitled *Violino Solo,* with works from J. S. Bach on up to the mid-twentieth century, including, of course, the great fugue movement of Bartok's solo violin sonata.

One day during my senior year, Professor Gross told me, point-blank: "Mr. Matus, you have talent, but you are lacking in self-confidence." Spurred to even greater effort by his words, I plowed ahead, aiming to finish with all "A"s in my music classes. After the summer in Waikiki with my mother, I returned to face my senior year. All went well: highest marks in everything, and Tony came to my graduation, bringing his camera to immortalize his brilliant son attired in academic robes (which I was delighted to wear, given their origin in monastic garb). Clara sent her best wishes for my future graduate studies, which she supposed I would begin during the coming fall semester, and she sent me a plane ticket to Honolulu, to spend the summer with her.

Chapter 18

Yet the previous summer in Honolulu, something powerful had happened to me—something that had changed the course of my life. I had accustomed myself to early-morning and evening sitting meditations, grounded in the Kriya-Yoga practice as taught by Yogananda and his direct disciples. I usually focused my attention on an icon, which showed the line of gurus as Yogananda had envisioned them, with Jesus in the center, at his right the mythical hermit of the Himalayas, Babaji, and at Babaji's right, Swami Sriyukteswar, Yogananda's guru. To the left of Jesus was Lahiri Mahasaya, Sriyukteswar's guru, and at his left, the last of the lineage, Yogananda himself. Though in recent years, SRF began selling an altered icon, with Krishna to the right of Jesus—which of course means that Jesus is placed to the left of Krishna—I really do not think that Yogananda would have permitted this change.

One evening during my sitting meditation in my mother's apartment, an easy walk away from a dormant volcano called "Diamond Head," I reflected on the fact that I had never known Yogananda in the flesh (I missed receiving his personal blessing by less than four years). But I did remember my first contact with SRF in 1957, the summer before I began my studies at Oxy. Walking up the hill to the SRF headquarters, I found the gate open and took a few steps onto the grounds, and a man maybe ten years older than me introduced himself as Leland Standing. He asked if I had read the *Autobiography of a Yogi.* I told him I had and that I wanted to practice Kriya Yoga meditation. He informed me that he was the very last disciple received by the late Master in person. I realized that, given this one degree of separation from Yogananda, I felt as close to the guru as was possible, since he was no longer on this earthly plane.

Still in meditation, the thought came to me that I needed a spiritual teacher of my own. I said to myself: "I need a guru." At that instant I heard a voice, not loud but quite clear, and not identifiable as the voice of any person I knew. The voice said to me: "The Catholic Church is your guru."

I realized that the voice had come from heaven, and that the words were absolutely true, and that I was called to respond immediately and freely. I realized that for me there was no alternative but to follow the voice, and not just with an inner movement of my soul. So, I resolved to call the Catholic Diocese of Honolulu in the morning and to make an appointment with a priest, who would tell me how I could become a Catholic. The next Sunday I attended my first Mass as a believer in Christ's real presence in the bread and wine on the altar. For the time being my communion—since I had not yet received the Catholic sacraments—was a "communion of desire." However, for one such as myself, Catholic theology promises a grace equivalent to receiving the consecrated host.

Waikiki's parish church, built perhaps in the early twentieth century, was a modest structure in latticework that let the trade winds breathe gently on those attending Mass. It was dedicated to Saint Augustine, the north-African mystic and theologian, himself an adult convert to Catholic Christianity. The liturgy, as was then the custom, was entirely in Latin, but after proclaiming the New Testament readings in the language of ancient Rome, the priest read them in English, and I heard the gospel text in which Jesus tells the parable of the lost sheep. It seemed as if the reading had been chosen to welcome me, a sheep now safe within the sheepfold, as a new "Catholic of desire." After the Mass, I stood for a few minutes outside the chapel to look at the large statue of Saint Augustine, and I silently addressed him: "You were a convert; I am a convert; pray for me!" And I walked back to my mother's apartment.

I ought to have foreseen that an interior tempest would follow this instantaneous conversion, a tempest of winds from opposite horizons, sometimes overwhelming me with a fearful uncertainty about my ability to hold fast to Catholicism, and then, at other times, bringing me to a quiet place in my soul, where I knew that God was with me, loving me tenderly and unconditionally and guiding me toward the Church and whatever my new vocation might be.

My meeting with the priest at the Catholic cathedral in downtown Honolulu went as well as it could, though by intuition I knew that he was unsure how to address my eagerness to receive the sacraments and my ardent will to affirm the Church's doctrines. He asked me whether I lived in Hawaii, and I told him that I was about to begin my senior year at Occidental College. He was visibly relieved and encouraged me to think everything over once I was back in California, and to find a priest there willing to give me instruction in the faith. I realize how I must have appeared to him: a smart young man attending a rich kids' college, who was trying to impress a priest with his intellectual conservatism and his firm adherence to defined dogmas.

Chapter 19

As for my mother, the abrupt change of my posture during morning meditation—from the lotus posture to kneeling at the bedside—was certainly noticed by her, but she was neither troubled nor curious. Once again, I surmised that Clara intuitively understood what was happening in her son's soul. I came to accept the contrasting winds of scrupulous self-questioning and self-consoling piety. However, I did not just believe that I was a believer; I knew with quiet certitude that God had infused true faith into my soul, and my turning to the Catholic Church had set me on the right path, where my task was simply to keep walking, in spite of the complex emotions that surfaced in my psyche, whether they were scrupulous fears of this or that sin or my obsessive intellectual difficulties with regard to creeds and disciplines that cradle Catholics serenely take to heart as if they were family heirlooms.

Many persons who have suddenly embraced the faith of the Roman Catholic Church have affirmed that, as they journeyed into their new faith, they realized that they had always been Catholics. I am not certain I could say the same of myself, although it was of primary importance for me to recognize the fact that the withdrawal of both my parents from the respective teachings and customs of their religious upbringing was an important factor in my own relations with institutional religion in general. Whether I was a disciple of guru Yogananda or a devout and practicing Catholic, I needed the humility of a true convert and the necessary patience with the inner process of conversion, which is all grace, all God's doing in my soul. It was critical that my belonging to the Catholic Church could never be subsumed under the rubric of ideology.

I was very drawn to my grandmother's sweet, Polish-Catholic devotion. I know very little about my grandfather's life of faith—only that he learned to tolerate the matrimonial instability of most of his children and also accepted the decision of my grandmother to exclude him from her bedroom. So perhaps my father's withdrawal from religious practice did not stem from anything his parents imposed on him but was rooted in the rigid mindset of the priests who had instructed him and his siblings, a rigidity which at the end left young Tony terrified.

The only one of his five siblings who stayed married to the same woman and at least occasionally attended Sunday Mass was my Uncle John, the youngest of the three Matus boys; his wife Marjorie was of German ancestry with a strong personality, totally committed to family life and to regular Sunday Mass. Uncle John loved Aunt Marge, but neither of the other two Matus brothers adored the one woman in his life as much as Tony adored my mother, despite their divorce. And after Clara embraced Catholicism while I was a novice at the Big Sur hermitage, I realized that the Church's teachings on the sacraments were only strengthening her resolve not to marry again until after Tony had passed from this life. "I do not feel I am unmarried," she said to me and to the priest who was instructing her in the Catholic faith.

Given the various ways that religion affected my family members, I have to say that the Catholicism I embraced at the age of twenty was not very different from their inherited Catholicism. For me, all of it was the gift of a loving God. I understood the Catholic Church as my authentic and ultimate teacher, that is, my guru, while for the Matus family the Church was very much their mother. The first divine gift to my soul, that is, my free choice of attending Baptist Sunday School and my receiving baptism at the hands of the Rev. Dr. Boyce Van Osdell did not make me a strict Baptist. There was, of course, a brief phase of evangelical fervor while I attended Sunday School, but by the age of thirteen I had ceased my attendance, once other interests—mainly yoga and classical music—had come to occupy my mind and heart.

Chapter 20

After my conversion and during the last half of my senior year at Occidental College, I made a retreat at the recently founded Camaldolese hermitage in Big Sur. It was 1961, I was twenty-one, and I thought I might have a possible vocation to their contemplative order. Having left Yogananda's Self-Realization Fellowship (SRF), I was now attending daily Mass instead, and in the way I'd once been drawn to the life of a Hindu renunciate, I now found myself drawn to the monastic life as found within Catholicism. I sincerely desired to profess vows of stability, reformation of my life and obedience according to the Rule of Saint Benedict. At the same time, I was hearing the obsessive question in my mind, "Am I going to make it as a monk?"

This meant, "Will I be able to observe stability?" This is the monk's first vow, according to the Benedictine Rule.

When I first set foot on the grounds of New Camaldoli Hermitage after a risky drive north from Los Angeles by way of Highway 1, I felt I was on the true path and was convinced that I must live Saint Benedict's monastic vow of stability as a promise to "keep on going." The greatest impediment to practicing this good conviction was my obsessive perfectionism. This was not, I now think, a sure sign of a novice's fervor, that is, it was not yet the "good zeal" praised by Saint Benedict. But sometimes you can make up for your lack of true virtue if you keep on doing whatever, at any given moment, you are able to do and that your conscience allows or prods you to do. There may be some "bitter zeal" mixed with the good, but in Catholic morality and in the Benedictine Rule, you learn by doing what you can in each moment.

My first lesson in holy obedience came after my retreat, when the prior told me I should take a year of discernment before returning to the hermitage.

This year would give me time to truly think through the step I was already convinced I must take.

I knew quite well that most candidates for religious life or the priesthood have on their minds not the challenge of stability but the matter of the sixth and ninth commandments—for Catholics and Lutherans these are the commandments that guide one's sex life and that condemn reading pornography and frequenting prostitutes, or, for those who are married, betraying one's spouse. Still on the same level of gravity, these commandments also forbid the act of "playing with yourself," as my mother called it. In the Catechism and in most interpretations of Catholic doctrine, every single act against the sixth and the ninth commandments is an objectively grave sin.

This clear and consistent Catholic teaching *de sexto et nono* was and still is affirmed to be unchangeable, and indeed that it is a unanimous teaching of the New Testament and the Fathers of the Church, including the medieval mystics as well. The Church's magisterium affirms that the saving deeds and words of Jesus are efficacious always and everywhere, and for anyone of good will, whatever Jesus commands us to do is indeed doable and benefits us greatly. In the face of this clarity and consistency (and I might include the severity and intransigence that a fragile and scrupulous soul might perceive behind the Church's reasonable arguments), I felt that my only recourse was to accept the teaching and to keep silence, except in the confessional, where everything I might have done, or even thought of doing, that transgressed any of the commandments—and not only the sixth and the ninth—had to be honestly and precisely confessed. This teaching of the Church was clear and devoid of ambiguity, and I thought it should be quite easy for me to observe, were it not for the self-doubts that plagued me.

My quest to become a Camaldolese monk was forcing me to develop a different kind of mind, one that expressed more than the mental agility and eagerness of a talkative three-year-old or an all-too-smart nerd in high school and college.

PART TWO
THE CALL

Chapter 21

After graduation, I went to Honolulu to stay with my mother. She told me that I needed to get a job and share expenses with her, which I did willingly. I found ready employment as an assistant librarian at the high school and college run by the Marianist Brothers, and I also signed up for a course in Latin at the Catholic college, based on the new teaching system favored by Waldo Sweet, called "structuralist linguistics," which focused on the grammatical structures in 360 sentences as models for conveying meaning by way of Latin. The efficacy of this method was reinforced by my intense desire to prepare for a life of prayer centered in the Mass and in the Liturgy of the Hours, celebrated day and night in all Latin-rite monasteries of the Order of Saint Benedict.

When my year of discernment was up in June of 1962, I wrote a letter to Father Clemente Roggi, the prior in Big Sur, requesting the community's hospitality for a lengthy period of discernment at the hermitage. Then I boarded a flight from Honolulu to Los Angeles, spent one night with my father, and at dawn I started driving north. After several hours I recognized the winding dirt road leading up to the Hermitage. The first person I spoke to upon arriving was again the resident layman, Michael Murphy, whom I had met on arriving for my spur-of-the-moment visit the previous year. He directed me to the prior's cell. I told prior Fr. Roggi, and novice master Fr. Joseph Diemer that I was here for a week and were I to be accepted into the program of monastic formation, I would be willing to stay indefinitely. At the end of my retreat, they welcomed me as a candidate for monastic vows at New Camaldoli.

At the hermitage there were no other candidates present at that time, except for a lay-brother postulant. The first group of "choir-monk" candidates had left for the four-year program in theology at the Pontifical Benedictine University in Rome (Sant'Anselmo on the Aventine Hill). They would soon profess their solemn vows and then be ordained at the mother house of Camaldoli during their fourth year. Having concluded their studies, they would return immediately to New Camaldoli. Since I had barely gotten to know them before they left Big Sur, I was eager to see them again, so that we might collaborate in making New Camaldoli a truly American hermitage. There were also four in the group that began to form after I arrived.

I met privately with Fr. Joseph, and he asked me about the latest books I had read. Of course, I named a couple of classics of monastic literature, but then he asked me, "What would someone who comes to a monastery or a hermitage be looking for?"

I answered, "Well, Father, my answer may be too simple, but I think the goal of monastic life is union with God by charity."

Fr. Joseph's face brightened with a smile. "That's it: union with God by love!" (I appreciated the subtle nuance of his preferring the word "love" to the Latin-derived term "charity"). And he added, "An essential part of your formation will include the writings of the great mystics, like Teresa of Avila and John of the Cross." Since these two saints were on my reading list already, I was glad that their writings were part of the program, even though the two saints were Carmelites, rather than Benedictines.

After a month at the hermitage, the monks accepted my request to be clothed in the white robe girded with a white woolen sash, the basic habit for postulants who would be preparing for priestly ordination as well as for monastic consecration. The first major monastic feast after my arrival was the solemnity of Saint Benedict, celebrated on July 11 with a solemn high Mass and Vespers in Gregorian Chant. There I was clothed in the tunic and received a white woolen cape without a hood.

While still living in one of the old cabins of what used to be a dude ranch, I was visited by Fr. Joseph, who continued to guide us after we had made our first or "simple" vows. He told me explicitly that the cenobitic tradition—the monastic practice of community living—was an essential element in Camaldolese formation. "You won't get to be a hermit unless you are first a good cenobite," said Fr. Joseph. I felt deep relief, hearing the strong encouragement in these words of our novice master, who had always emphasized "silence and solitude" as a necessary requisite for the real mystical experience of God. Just short of a year later I was vested as a novice with the full Camaldolese habit: a tunic bound by the woolen sash, then a long scapular that hung down to the hem of the tunic, and a detached *cappuccio* or double hood covering the shaven scalp that showed a "crown," that is, a narrow strip of short hair that circled around the back of the head.

Chapter 22

My first full year in the Big Sur Hermitage coincided with the first session of the Second Vatican Council, which seemed to promise well for the *aggiornamento* ("updating") of the Church's canon law and for the liturgy, and above all for the renewal of our fundamental understanding of faith as a devout people's humble journey guided by God's grace and the Church's teachings. One of the outstanding *periti* ("expert advisors") at the service of the bishops and abbots, who were the voting members of the Council, was a Benedictine monk and a widely-esteemed expert on liturgy, dom Cipriano Vagaggini, who made important contributions to the outline and text of *Sacrosanctum Concilium,* the first "constitution" or major document of the Council, the one that granted to parishes and religious communities of the Roman Rite the faculty of using the living languages (English, Italian *et al)* in the celebration of the Mass and the other sacraments.

In the years immediately following Vatican 11, as I was pursuing a graduate degree in theology at the Pontifical University of Sant'Anselmo in Rome, dom Vagaggini was one of my professors, and after his retirement from the faculty, he transferred his monastic vow of stability to the Hermitage and Monastery of Camaldoli, which was not far from his birthplace in Tuscany.

The canonical year as a novice, which was required for admission to simple vows as a Camaldolese Benedictine monk, was to be the full three hundred and sixty-five days following our clothing in the complete habit. But the actual date was June 19, 1965, the solemnity of Saint Romuald: two days short, but so what? Forward march! You're a monk now, I told myself, bound to the vows of stability, reformation of life and obedience (the actual rite also added the words "poverty and chastity" to the vows for simple profession). This was now my calling and the life I had chosen to live, until God should call me to my eternal reward. Fr. Joseph had made it clear that we had better be sure of our willingness to move forward as monks and get ready to pronounce those solemn perpetual vows at the end of the three years in simple vows.

Let me add to those words of Fr. Joseph the awareness that had come to me following my public profession of vows: I was here, and to be happy I must stay—as simple as that, and it was always there in the background, even when I was assailed by scruples and worries about the gravity of my sins, and was obsessed with anxious questions having no answer other than the Latin phrase *Promitto stabilitatem meam,* "I promise my stability."

The hermitage had been a construction site since its inception in 1958, and now the building of the two rows of cells on the ocean side of the property was almost finished. Once the cells were ready, we moved in. The vision of the vast Pacific that confronted me as I stepped out my door was all but overwhelming, but not fearsome for me. The underlying fear that still saddled me was the fear of forgetting my strong personal motivations for becoming a Catholic and for entering New Camaldoli to become a monk of the Order of Saint Benedict. I knew that anything could happen to any one of us (as later did happen to the brothers who took vows with me, in a way that I could not have foreseen), but with "fear and trembling" I moved forward without looking back. I knew that this was not just a choice on my part. It was first and always God's call—God had chosen to call me. I did not presume to have the strength or the constancy to "tough it out," since by nature and temperament I was anything but tough, just stubborn. Of course, stubbornness was also not enough, but it would have to do for now.

What my convert scruples did not permit me to recognize was the abiding influence on me of Yogananda and the yogis of India. Theirs were simpler ceremonies and in some ways, they practiced a simpler lifestyle than we did as Benedictine monks. But my silent meditations practiced at New Camaldoli, with a volume of Gregorian Chant on my lap as I chanted the Latin phrases like mantras, were a baptized expression of the actual grace of India that was still with me.

So, by God's grace and with my abiding intention of doing God's will, my Christian, Catholic and Benedictine practice still resonated, to a certain degree, with the ideal of yoga as transmitted to me by the *Autobiography of a Yogi* and the sacrificial rite of breathing that Yogananda's correspondence course and my instruction by Brahmachari Leland had taught me. While I was a junior monk at New Camaldoli, I also reconnected with Donald Walters (formerly known as Brother Kriyananda).

After serving as vice-president of Self Realization Fellowship, he was asked to leave their Mother-Center, and had just arrived at New Camaldoli, seeking a private retreat in complete silence and solitude, in order to find where God was drawing him. Donald still remembered me, and our brother in charge of guests asked me to go speak with him. I imagined that he was seeking a way of rebuilding his life as a Christian (he had been raised Episcopalian), and I brought him a few books that I hoped would answer his questions. Soon he moved on and found some people who supported his idea of a new community of devotees, initiated into the meditation practices of Paramhansa Yogananda but less closed and severe than what, in his eyes, SRF had become.

Chapter 23

During my first five years at New Camaldoli, the prior and the novice master guided us through the obligatory courses in Latin, Greek and scholastic philosophy, largely focused on the principles that sustained the theological tradition of the Roman Church from the Middle Ages onward. In first place was the *Summa Theologiae* of St. Thomas Aquinas. And lest we be troubled by the idea that the *Summa* was "Dominican theology," we were reminded that Aquinas had received an important part of his education from the Benedictine monks of Monte Cassino. We also studied Gregorian Chant, which we sang at least on Sundays, solemnities and major feast days, provoking occasional grumbling about "all that singing" from the priests who had come from the diocesan clergy or missionary congregations to "join the hermits." I was grateful that both the prior and the novice master held fast to their own formation, solidly grounded in Catholic liturgical prayer and Saint Benedict's Holy Rule.

The classes in Latin, Greek and philosophy paralleled our preparation for solemn monastic vows which, under the new Camaldolese Constitutions, were to be professed in the house of one's stability, in our case, at New Camaldoli. On June 19, 1967, there were four of us at the altar of the Big Sur hermitage, each one promising individually, one after the other, our lifetime commitment to "Stability, Reformation of my life, and Obedience, according to the Rule of our Holy Father Benedict and the Camaldolese Constitutions, in the Camaldolese Congregation of the Order of Saint Benedict, at Immaculate Heart Hermitage in Big Sur, California." Three brothers of the first group of newly professed American Camaldolese soon returned from Rome, and I was glad that they would be here to serve the community.

Shortly thereafter, I and my companions in vows left for Italy. A friend of the Hermitage was the owner of an airline that specialized in chartered flights from California to Europe, and he offered us seats on an empty plane being sent to Europe to bring a group of Americans home. The flight landed in Paris, and since I was moderately fluent in French, I was able to reserve seats for us on a night train that would bring us to Florence the following morning.

Upon arriving in Italy, I had to dive into another language—Italian—and having the phone number of Camaldoli, I called the Hermitage and announced to the brother at the Eremo our arrival at the central train station in Firenze. I understood the brother's reply—"Restate la!"—correctly surmising that it meant "Stay there!" I stood for more than an hour outside the entrance to the station, until a man not much older than me walked up and asked me, in English, "Are you American?" We were welcomed at Camaldoli by dom Aliprando Catani, our saintly prior general, and he himself drove us up to the Holy Hermitage. Our arrival there was just before August 15, the solemnity of the Assumption of Mary, popularly called "Ferragosto" in Italy, a national holiday for family picnics and games. We were at the Eremo until late September, when we traveled to our monastery in Rome: San Gregorio al Celio, dedicated to St. Gregory the Great, who was the first monk to serve the Church as pope, and the author of the *Life of Saint Benedict.*

The seasons in the Tuscan Apennines, at more than 1,000 meters (ca. 3,600 feet) above sea level and at a latitude closer to Southern Canada than to Southern California, were different from the seasons in Big Sur, as I had lived them for the last four years, but I enjoyed the European equivalent of "Indian Summer," known in Italy as *'estate di san Martino* ("Saint Martin's summer," or "Martinmas" in English), which offered us mostly clear and even warm days, perhaps a brief rain in the evening, and as yet no ice or snow.

But the late September climate at our motherhouse in the Apennines could only be compared with New England: chilly, even when the sun was shining, and always very cold at night. I consoled myself with the probability of finding in Rome a climate like the one to which I was accustomed in Hollywood and San Bernardino, which allowed palm trees to flourish, along with Saint-John's-Bread trees, with their sweet carob pods. I had tasted them from a tree in our back yard on Broadlawn Drive, and two decades later, I found a whole grove of them, just a short walk from our monastery of San Gregorio in Rome.

Chapter 24

We American Camaldolese, together with the Italian brothers studying theology in the same classes, arrived at Rome's central train station and took a subway to the stop nearest to the Camaldolese church of San Gregorio, so near that when we emerged from the subway station, we were looking directly toward the facade of the monastery. Mindful of the chaotic traffic, we crossed the street, and one of the monks residing at San Gregorio, don Bonifacio Filippetti, waved to us from a third-story window. When we entered the courtyard, Bonifacio was already at the entrance to the monks' cloister. He opened the door for us and said, *"Avrete fame! Venite al refettorio e troverete tutto pronto."* Immediately I recognized the essential words: *fame* [FAH-meh] (hunger) and *pronto* [PRONE-toh] (ready). With a gesture, he invited us to follow him down a small flight of stairs that brought us to the refectory. We had been very well fed at the Sacro Eremo, and here we saw a rich spread of warm pasta, cooked vegetables, meat, salad greens and fresh fruit. And wine, of course, the usual tawny white wine from the vineyards outside Rome.

Vespers and Compline (Evening prayer and Night prayer) were perfectly familiar to me—I had been chanting them in Latin since I joined New Camaldoli—although on ordinary weekdays in Big Sur our "chanting" was *recto tono,* chanting on a single note and at a very slow pace. But every day the monks at San Gregorio sang the authentic Gregorian melodies, as published by the monk—scholars of the Abbey of Solesmes in France, and this was just as one would expect, in a church dedicated to the memory of Pope Gregory the Great, to whom the melodies of Christian psalmody were legendarily ascribed (although there is no documentary evidence of Saint Gregory's being himself a cantor).

A good response to a call from God is itself a pure, free gift of God. All is grace. The Catholic Mass and the Church in the early Sixties were pouring out grace on many souls then, and—let me say it again— the greatest grace was the Second Vatican Council, called by Saint John XXIII and presided over by him during its entire first session. That session offered us the *Constitution on the Sacred Liturgy,* to whose text and theological grounding our own monk, Father Cipriano Vagaggini, had made a great contribution. All the other reforms initiated and promoted by Vatican II, in their theological and spiritual orientation, flow from the liturgy constitution, that is, from the prayer of the Church. And the Vatican II liturgy is and continues to be our ordinary prayer as members of the Roman Church, the faithful continuation of the liturgy as celebrated by the first monk-pope, Saint Gregory the Great in the sixth century. This is, and must continue to be, the prayer of the Roman Church, and we monks can do no better, in this twenty-first century, than to practice our vow of stability as monks of Vatican II by faithfully celebrating the Council's liturgy in the language of the people.

Here, I need to add a few words about the brothers who were with me at the altar as we professed our solemn perpetual vows, and with whom I then traveled to Italy to continue our studies. Sad to say, less than three years after pronouncing their vows and completing their theological education, all three of them—each for different and uniquely personal reasons—felt the need to abandon the Camaldolese life, and the one priest among them, Abel *[pseudonym],* ceased to exercise his ministry. He had met a woman with whom he had fallen in love, and they were content to marry in a civil ceremony. I did my best to banish from my mind any and all judgmental thoughts about these brothers. I realized that I could not claim any great virtue for the fact of my perseverance, which I attribute solely to God's mercy and all-powerful grace; to a much lesser degree I also attribute it to my innate stubbornness.

We were not the first Americans to pronounce solemn vows: four other American Camaldolese had preceded us, and all but one of them were in a hurry to finish their exams in Rome and to return as soon as possible to the hermit life at Big Sur. Of this first group of American Camaldolese, Fr. Robert Hale was an exception in many ways. He was no less a contemplative than the others, but he had a cheerful spirit and bonded quickly with young men who joined the community. He was an ideal master for the novices and junior monks. Health reasons obliged him to remain in Rome when the others returned to the Big Sur Hermitage, and he also requested the permission of the Prior General to enroll in the doctoral program in theology at Fordham University in New York. Robert's older brother had maintained a trust fund for him that would completely cover his tuition fees and any other expenses. This request had already been made while Robert was a monk in simple vows in Big Sur, and soon after his ordination to the priesthood, he entered the Ph.D. program at Fordham, specializing in the spirituality of Pierre Teilhard de Chardin, a Jesuit paleontologist, philosopher and mystical theologian.

After three years, at the end of the Camaldolese general chapter that had prepared new constitutions for our monastic congregation, each of the monks was ordered to choose one of the five larger Camaldolese communities as their respective "house of stability" or permanent residence. Robert chose the mother-house in Italy—the Holy Hermitage and Monastery of Camaldoli—and so did I. The community in Italy had no difficulty in granting me permission to study for my doctorate at Fordham University in New York. My tuition fees were paid for by scholarships that had been granted to me on the basis of my high grade point average from Occidental College and my *summa cum laude* degree in theology from Sant'Anselmo, the Benedictine theological faculty in Rome. Other expenses were covered by my ministry to a community of nursing sisters from Quebec.

As a monk of the Holy Hermitage and Monastery of Camaldoli, I had the option of choosing which of the two houses to live in. I chose the monastery. I took care, however, to spend no less than two or three weeks at the Eremo every year. It so happened that I am the only American among the Camaldolese to have spent an entire winter at the Holy Hermitage (snow and ice galore!). There was a peaceful atmosphere in both houses, and all the monks were addressing each other by their monastic or baptismal name, without a title, although I hesitated to address the older Italian monks with such informality; for years they were still *"Padre"* for me.

Chapter 25

It was significant for us all that the new Constitutions had eliminated any and all distinctions of clerical status, except those intrinsically connected with the sacramental ministry, through which the priests served the community and its guests. All shared in the common tasks for the upkeep of the monastery and for the Liturgy of the Hours, taking turns in leading the daily Offices of prayer. On the other hand, brothers who were not priests rendered many services connected with the guest ministry at Camaldoli. In addition, my full immersion in daily community life enabled me to perfect my fluency in Italian, and after three years or so, I was grateful to hear compliments about my good pronunciation and idiomatic use of the language. Finding myself at home with the Italian language also reinforced my sense of belonging to the monastery of Camaldoli, my place of *stabilitas,* more my home than even New Camaldoli in California, the state where I was born and the hermitage I had initially joined.

A significant grace connected with my stable residence at the Cenobium of Camaldoli was the call to teach at the Benedictine theological faculty of Sant'Anselmo in Rome. Robert was also teaching there, but he preferred to live at our student monastery of San Gregorio al Celia, in the heart of ancient Rome, while I commuted from Camaldoli during the semesters when I taught. My courses centered on the interreligious dialogue mandated by the Second Vatican Council.

The theme of each course varied from year to year, so it was appropriate for students personally engaged in dialogue to take my course twice. I always returned to Camaldoli immediately after the exams. I had learned to love my cell in the *Cenobio di Camaldoli* (also called *Fontebono,* "Good Wellspring"), and there I followed Saint Romuald's admonition, *"Sede in eel/a quasi in paradiso":* "Sit in your cell as if you were in heaven." The cell was indeed a paradise for an avid reader like me and—with a cassette recorder and later with its successor devices—an avid listener to twentieth-century classical music.

Another grace of my residing at Fontebono was my meeting of minds and a shared love of music with don Graziano Mengozzi, born just beyond the crest of the Apennines, to the north-east of the Sacro Eremo. He was in his teens when I was born and had been a novice with the monks of Camaldoli at the precise moment when the monks called on expert organ builders to install pipe organs in both our churches—at the Eremo first, then at the Cenobio. Graziano was sent to study at *Musica Sacra,* the most important school of liturgical music in Italy and perhaps in the world. When I met him, he was residing permanently at the Cenobio, was *maestro* ("master") of the organist's art, and *padrone* ("master" or "owner") of the organ itself, but he was always hospitable to other organists, if they were well trained.

As for music, my training in this art had not prepared me for the composition of liturgical music. In terms of accompaniment, the first chapel at New

Camaldoli, which occupied an old truck garage, had a small organ at which I would freeze up the few times I attempted to accompany Gregorian chant. At the monastery of Camaldoli, guitar accompaniment was offered at occasional Masses for youth groups by don Giacomo Calabresi, a *pugliese* [pool-YEH-zeh] monk (that is, one born in Apulia, close to the "heel" of the Italian "boot"); he was two years my senior but for some reason had not yet been ordained (he was eventually ordained a few months before I was). He was also a good organist, skilled at improvising chordal accompaniment to Gregorian chant. Don Innocenzo Gargano was another pugliese and best friend of Giacomo during their middle school education with the Camaldolese and their years studying Catholic philosophy and theology in Rome. Although not trained in instrumental music, don Innocenzo was gifted not only in Gregorian chant but also, with Giacomo's organ accompaniment, to an Italian equivalent of "Catholic folk-rock," in the vein of the American vocalists Peter, Paul and Mary.

However, since the Innocenzo-Giacomo duo were too deeply immersed in the life of the monastic community, and Innocenzo in his study of medieval Greek Orthodox theology, to focus on their liturgical singing, they chose the ministries of preaching and teaching. At this point, don Emanuele, as our chief liturgist and assistant to don Benedetto, called on me to begin gathering together the existing melodies for our Liturgy of the Hours and for the Mass "propers," that is, the short liturgical phrases, proper to specific saints or seasons, sung at Mass and during the hours of the Divine Office. But he also wanted me to complete the repertoire with new melodies to provide our communities with sufficient resources in Italian for chanting the liturgical Hours and the Masses of the entire Church calendar. Since the amount of music already composed was still far from sufficient, Emanuele gave me full encouragement to add whatever was needed, in order to celebrate in song the entire liturgical year.

Chapter 26

The best resource for unison melodies was in Gregorian chant itself, and so the Camaldolese at the Eremo and the Cenobium, as well as in our other Italian houses, wanted the change of language to continue echoing the Gregorian rhythm. On my own I had studied Gregorian chant and sang it decently at New Camaldoli and at our motherhouse in Italy during the last seven years in which the Camaldolese were still celebrating the Divine Office and Mass in Latin. As soon as the Council had affirmed the pastoral value of using the language of the people in liturgical prayer, I set to work, welcoming any contributions of words and melodies which other musically and/or poetically gifted brothers offered to the community, in view of the publication of a *Salterio,* a repertoire of melodies to enrich the prayer of the Psalms and other liturgical poetry, always in the light of the paschal mystery of the crucified and risen Jesus, together with the gift of the Holy Spirit.

So that the daily fruits of my labor might be available for all, for their comments and for the correction of any errors, I set up an Apple computer and a printer in a reading room at the monastery, always accessible to the monks. Another monk, who edited *Vita monastica,* our Camaldolese quarterly publication, was working in the same room every day. The door was always open, and the actual printed copies of the daily production of melodies were on a table at the center of the room. I invited everyone to make suggestions and indicate whatever needed correcting, and I continued to work, under pressure from the Catholic publishing house that already had other Camaldolese books in their catalogue. And, quite frankly, I also was eager to see our liturgical project in print as soon as possible, because I had other services to perform, especially in the dialogue of Christians with devotees of other religious traditions. Thus, the desire on various sides to accelerate the project motivated me to focus my days on bringing the *Salterio* to conclusion.

Finally, our book of liturgical music was accepted and was sent to the printer, and the Italian publisher delivered to our bookstores the *Salterio monastico, canto e preghiera,* "A monastic psalter, song and prayer," in a quantity sufficient for the use of our monks at the Eremo and the Cenobio and for our guests at Camaldoli. One evening after supper, Don Emanuele presented the book to the community with a few words, and having found a misprint in one of the introductory pages, indicated the page number and the correct reading and said no more. Some grumbling followed, and after we had said grace, our organist don Graziano showed a dour face, and the following day he asked me why I had not shown him the project before sending it to the publisher. I reminded him that every day the newly drafted pages had been available on the table in our workplace for corrections and comments. Above all, the haste in my completing the work was in response to the demands of the publisher and was, I thought, in keeping with don Emanuele's orders.

In the following days and weeks, many letters arrived, full of praise for our *Salterio.* The letters were addressed to don Benedetto and don Emanuele, and many were from the superiors of other Benedictine monasteries of monks and nuns. As we began to use the new book, I guided the guests and retreatants at the monastery in singing the new melodies with the monks, and the results were gratifying. Don Graziano used his perfect mastery of modal harmony to accompany the new psalmody at the organ, and I could hear in his accompaniment a relaxation of the tension between us that had arisen upon my presentation of the finished *Salterio.*

At each successive liturgy, the "new" music of the *Salterio*—echoing as it did the modes and especially the rhythm of Gregorian chant as published by the monks of Solesmes (soh-LEM] Abbey in France—became easier and easier to sing, not only for the monks but also for those friends and guests who had previously participated in our Latin chanting at Camaldoli. A few years later, an English version of the *Salterio monastico* was prepared and published as a joint project with my dear colleague and confrere at New Camaldoli, don Cyprian Consiglio.

Chapter 27

As a direct consequence of my finishing the *Salterio* project for our communities, I felt strongly drawn in the direction of our Camaldolese brothers in the U.S.A. No one expressly invited me to return, but it seemed that the door was open, and that it would be good for me to try settling back into Big Sur or Berkeley. For more than twenty years, our original motherhouse at Camaldoli in Tuscany had been my home, even though I was also a frequent presence at our younger foundation in Brazil, and especially at Shantivanam, our Benedictine Ashram in India, where I shared with the monastic sisters and brothers my knowledge of the Camaldolese Benedictine heritage, with a few words about the phase of my own journey under the influence of Hindu spirituality as transmitted by Paramhansa Yogananda. Soon I realized that our Christian Ashrams in India—solidly grounded in the sacraments of the Catholic Church and in the teachings of her great mystics and saints—were much more authentically Indian than the Self-Realization Fellowship communities in Hollywood, on Mount Washington and elsewhere in the United States.

However, I do acknowledge the value of Yogananda's bringing yoga meditation to the West—a resource for me personally, from which I have freely drawn, and which ultimately enabled me to bear fruit in my life as a contemplative Christian monk in California and Italy. And, of course, I do hope that my periods at our Benedictine ashram in India have honored the teachings and the contemplative witness of Jules Monchanin, Henri Le Saux and Bede Griffiths, the founders of Shantivanam ("forest of peace"), the historic Christian ashram in Tamil Nadu, which is the largest state in the Indian Federation.

The ashram lives on, both at its original location and elsewhere on Indian soil, and I can say with conviction that the Christian monks and nuns there—the novices no less than the elder *sannyasis* and *sannyasinis*—continue with authenticity the life, example and teachings of the founders. In their insights, enriched by all that is best in India's great spiritual heritage, we find an abiding *evangelion,* a perennial Good News of what Jesus Christ, who is human like us in all things but sin, has done through them, and by the direct working of the Holy Spirit, who breathes within every wind that circles our planet and directly brings light to the people of India with their vast spiritual heritage.

The Yogananda I knew, at my one degree of separation from him, was the author of the first edition—now in the public domain—of the *Autobiography of a Yogi.* The chapters added later and other changes in the original text, together with the expanded footnotes, were not in the first edition. The "higher doctrine" of the added chapters and notes was, I felt, a departure from the original intention of Yogananda's syncretism—understanding the term "syncretism" not in the pejorative sense of mixing religious doctrines of various origin with little regard for the truth, but rather as an essentially Hindu way of sustaining peaceful relations with others, including those whose spiritual heritage is not rooted in the Vedas. Thus conceived, "syncretism" is a Hindu's way of affirming that those adhering to other traditions are also, in their own way, faithful to the universal Truth as most Hindus conceive it, that is, as *Sat-Chit-Ananda,* "Being, Consciousness, Bliss." Hence, devout Hindus can affirm that non-Hindus, faithful to their own traditions, can also enjoy direct access to the *sanatana dharma,* "the ever-abiding Truth" of the Vedas.

Six years passed between my first reading of the *Autobiography of a Yogi* in 1954 and my instantaneous conversion in 1960 on hearing the Voice that said, "The Catholic Church is your guru." The truth is, that without Yogananda's translation of Hindu wisdom into terms that I and other Americans could understand, I might never have heard that voice and embraced the Church with the faith of a Catholic. In other words, I needed to study and practice the *praeparatio evangelica* of Yogananda to prepare my soul for the rest of my life as a Christian, a Catholic and a Camaldolese Benedictine monk. Thus, my conversion at Waikiki, in my mother's apartment, did not end my connection with the India of Yogananda; rather it brought me to the wellspring of Christian India, the only Asian nation to the east of the Holy Land that the Roman Church calls an "apostolic Church," having been founded by my patron saint, Thomas the Apostle.

By God's grace, I have traveled far and wide. A few years ago, however, I traveled back in time. I wanted to visit the place where I was born, the legendary Hollywood. I wanted to see once again the house on Broadlawn Drive, where I asked so many questions of my dear parents, Clara and Tony. I wanted to stand on the corner of Wilshire and La Brea, where Tony had his Matus Camera Supply Company, and I wanted to return to Mount Washington, the motherhouse of the Self-Realization Fellowship, where Yogananda lived his last years and where I meditated in the garden, his "temple of leaves." And finally, I wanted to visit Occidental College, where I studied the twelve-tone system of musical composition and thought about writing music for the movies—Occidental, so near to Saint Dominic's Parish, where I first received the sacraments of the Catholic Church.

As a child, learning for the first time about the journey undertaken by Abraham, I declared that I wanted to make a great journey of my own. By God's grace, I have made one.